Closing the Execution Gap

How Great Leaders and Their Companies Get Results

Richard Lepsinger

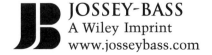

JOSSEY-BASS
A Wiley Imprint
www.josseybass.com

Published by Jossey-Bass
A Wiley Imprint
989 Market Street, San Francisco, CA 94103-1741—www.josseybass.com

Jossey-Bass books and products are available through most bookstores. To contact Jossey-Bass directly call our Customer Care Department within the U.S. at 800-956-7739, outside the U.S. at 317-572-3986, or fax 317-572-4002.

Jossey-Bass also publishes its books in a variety of electronic formats. Some content that appears in print may not be available in electronic books.

Library of Congress Cataloging-in-Publication Data
Lepsinger, Richard, 1948-
    Closing the execution gap : how great leaders and their companies get results / Richard Lepsinger. – 1st ed.
        p. cm.
    Includes bibliographical references and index.
    ISBN 978-0-470-53130-3 (cloth)
    1. Organizational effectiveness. 2. Performance. 3. Leadership. 4. Management. I. Title.
    HD58.9.L473 2010
    658–dc22

                                                                                    2010008641

Printed in the United States of America.
FIRST EDITION
HB Printing 10 9 8 7 6 5 4 3 2 1

Contents

List of Figures, Tables, and Exhibits

Acknowledgments

I'm grateful to many people for their help and support during the writing of this book. In particular I'd like to thank:

My partners Jennifer Forgie, who was the lead on the Execution Gap study and was instrumental in shaping the content of this book, and Darleen Derosa, whose suggestions and feedback were invaluable in helping refine and focus the chapters.

The people who deal with execution day-to-day and so generously shared their stories of success and failure: Anne Arni, Lee Bellarmino, Ken Berstein, Vicki Cansler, Nora Choi-Lee, Mary Eckenrod, Mike Festo, Harold Fink, Bernie Flynn, Tom Green, David Holland, Stan Hubbard, Marc Kaplan, Debbie Krauthiem, Mark Miller, Joe Napolitano, Kathi Saccullo, Steve Schloss, Joost Sytsma, Anna Trask, Gayle Weibley, Gary Weinstein, Melinda Wolfe, and Sean Woodroffe.

The people who agreed to review early drafts of the manuscript and provided insight and suggestions that helped make this a better book: Vince Baglio, Lee Bellarmino, Veronika Boesch, Debra Casey, Craig Dinsell, Ron Dukenski, Harold Fink, Bernie Flynn, Dan Forgie, Al Kieser, Toni Lucia, Mark Miller, Tom Rose, and Thaddeus Ward.

Dottie DeHart and her team at DeHart & Company, who were able to convert my technical, clinical writing style into something much more readable. And Max Wolfe, whose research was tremendously helpful.

And last, but certainly not least, my wife Bonnie Uslianer, who endured months of being a "book widow" while providing unconditional support and encouragement.

About the Author

Richard Lepsinger is president of OnPoint Consulting (www .onpointconsultingllc.com) and has a twenty-year track record of success as a human resource consultant and executive. He was a founder and managing partner of Manus, a human capital consulting firm, which he grew to over $4 million in revenue and sold to Right Management Consultants in 1998. At Right, Rick was the managing vice president of the Northeast and Eastern Canadian Consulting Practice, where he was responsible to fifty-five professionals and grew the region's revenue from $7 million to $20 million.

The focus of Rick's work has been on helping organizations close the gap between strategy and execution. He has served as a consultant to leaders and management teams at Astra-Zeneca, Bayer Pharmaceuticals, Citibank, Coca-Cola Company, Conoco-Philipps, Eisai Inc., GlaxoSmithKline, Goldman Sachs, Johnson & Johnson, KPMG, Merck & Co., the NYSE Euronext, Northwestern Mutual Life, PeopleSoft, Pfizer Inc., Pitney Bowes, Prudential, Siemens Medical Systems, Subaru of America, and UBS, among others.

Rick has extensive experience in formulating and implementing strategic plans, managing change, and talent management. He has addressed executive conferences and made presentations to leadership teams on the topics of leader effectiveness, strategy execution, managing change, performance management, 360-degree feedback and its uses, and developing and using competency models to enhance organizational performance.

Rick has co-authored three books on leadership, including *Flexible Leadership: Creating Value by Balancing Multiple Challenges and Choices* (with Dr. Gary Yukl), published by Jossey-Bass; *The Art and Science of 360-Degree Feedback* (2nd ed.; with Toni Lucia), published by Pfeiffer; and *The Art and Science of Competency Models* (with Toni Lucia), published by Pfeiffer.

He is also the author of several book chapters and articles on leadership and organizational effectiveness, including "Performance Management and Decision Making" in *The Handbook of Multisource Feedback*; and "Using 360-Degree Feedback in a Talent Management System" in *The Talent Management Handbook: Creating Organizational Excellence by Identifying, Developing, and Promoting Your Best People*. "Why Integrating the Leading and Managing Roles Is Essential for Organizational Effectiveness" (with Dr. Gary Yukl) appeared in *Organizational Dynamics* and is one of their most frequently downloaded articles.

Rick can be contacted at rlepsinger@onpointconsultingllc .com.

Introduction

If your company is like many companies, you may have a vision or mission statement about being number one in your industry...about your exceptional customer-driven service...about being a "one firm" firm. That's great. Having a shared picture of the kind of company you want to be provides something to strive for. But here's the real question: How true are these statements? How well are you delivering on your vision's promise?

In the past, the chasm between what's proudly proclaimed on your company website and reality might have been seen (and written off) as the standard "mission, vision, and values" statement that all companies feel obligated to produce. Even worse, it might have been joke fodder for customers and employees alike. But these days, it's just not funny anymore. If you can't execute in this sluggish economy (or any economy)—and execute well—you won't thrive. And there's a very real chance you won't survive.

We're living in unforgiving times. As I write these words, we're officially in "recovery," but experts warn of the possibility of a double-dip recession. Unemployment is hovering around 10 percent and consumers are clinging tightly to their wallets. Despite a hefty TARP infusion, banks are reluctant to lend. And many businesses are paralyzed by fear—fear of launching new products, entering new markets, buying new equipment, hiring staff, and taking the kinds of risks that can lead to prosperity and (ultimately) economic expansion.

This combination of frozen commercial credit, tight-fisted customers and general economic malaise has serious implications for businesses. They *must* be able to keep their promises to customers and shareholders and meet their goals. Execution has always been important, but when margins (and the margin for error) are paper thin, it's everything.

And that's why I wrote this book.

By the time you read this, economic conditions may have changed. Perhaps they'll have improved greatly or at least moderately. Perhaps they'll have stayed much the same. Or perhaps (and I sincerely hope this isn't the case) they'll be worse. Either way, execution will still matter, and the information in this book will still be relevant. And I think you'll see it's not the kind of information you'll find anywhere else.

As my company's recent study made clear—and as you will discover in the first chapter—the "conventional wisdom" about execution isn't all that wise. Most of us have been taught that if an organization has a clear vision and strategic direction, communicates that vision across the company, engages and motivates employees to achieve the vision, focuses on the customer, and provides quality products and services, success will surely follow. Unfortunately, this is not always the case.

In many companies, there is a deep and troubling gap between vision and strategy and actually "getting stuff done." What's worse, it appears many executives just don't believe their organizations can bridge that execution gap.

Although much attention has been focused on the need for organizations to improve their ability to execute, up until now, few specific, practical, research-based guidelines have been offered at the level of the day-to-day behavior it takes to get things done. Many of the current books on execution treat it as a "process" and focus on policy and procedure and organizational structure and systems. The implication is that you can "program" execution and that if you follow certain steps you will achieve the intended results.

Our research shows that "process" is only part of what it takes. This book is designed to fill that gap. It focuses on execution at the day-to-day operational level and describes what all managers (not just senior leaders) can do to ensure the delivery of consistent results. Unlike many of the books currently available, I will not only describe what needs to be done to enhance execution, but I will provide specific "how to" guidelines, tools, and skills for leaders.

This book is intended for anyone, at any level of the organization, who depends on others to get work done and is responsible for the successful implementation of plans and initiatives. Specifically, three groups will find this book particularly relevant and helpful:

- Leaders who manage a business, function, department, work unit, or team and are responsible for translating strategy into action and delivering results.
- Managers who do not have direct reports but need to coordinate across organizational boundaries to get work done.
- HR professionals who control many of the organizational systems required to support effective execution (hiring and selection, performance management, leadership development, rewards and recognition, and succession planning) and are responsible for ensuring leaders have the skills and knowledge needed to close the execution gap.

In addition, if you are dealing with one or more of the following situations, you will benefit from reading this book:

- You'd like to enhance your knowledge of execution in preparation for taking on a new role or implementing an important plan or initiative.
- You're preparing to take on additional responsibility as a result of a promotion.

- You'd like to enhance your ability to consistently implement plans and initiatives on time and on budget.
- You have an inconsistent track record in the delivery of business results.

The book is organized into seven chapters. Chapter One, "Vision Without Execution Is Hallucination," is a brief overview of the findings of my study of 409 companies from across industries. The baseline factors required for effective execution are briefly reviewed, and the majority of the chapter is spent on the five factors that differentiate companies that are most effective at executing plans and initiatives. Positive and negative examples of companies are provided for each differentiating factor. The rest of the book covers the specific things leaders can do—the Six Bridge Builders—to close the execution gap and help people get things done day-to-day.

Chapter Two, "Bridge Builder 1: Translate Strategy into Action," focuses on how to ensure a strong link and clear line of sight exists between strategy and vision, strategic projects and programs, and project action plans. Tools for action planning and techniques to help minimize risk and increase the likelihood of success are also provided.

Chapter Three, "Bridge Builder 2: Expect Top Performance," explains how and why your expectations of others and how you interact with them produces the level of performance, high or low, consistent with those expectations. I've included suggestions for how to set higher expectations for direct reports who have not performed well in the past and techniques for translating your higher expectations into high-impact behavior that will enhance your direct report's performance.

Chapter Four, "Bridge Builder 3: Hold People Accountable," reviews the reasons why people don't take accountability and why they feel the need to make excuses. It also explains why we don't consistently hold people accountable and why we should.

The chapter provides easy-to-use tools to help you manage accountability and increase the likelihood that your direct reports and team members will take responsibility for their actions and the impact of those actions.

Chapter Five, "Bridge Builder 4: Involve the Right People in Making the Right Decisions," describes the psychological and cognitive processes that impact how we process and react to information and that determine the choices we make. The factors that impact our judgment and the quality of our decisions are also explained. I've also provided practical techniques for avoiding the pitfalls of a lack of relevant information, poor information processing, impulsive reactions to what appear to be familiar situations, overly emotional responses, and risk aversion.

Chapter Six, "Bridge Builder 5: Facilitate Change Readiness," explains why it is so hard for us to change our behavior and what you can do to enhance your direct reports' and team members' readiness for change. What top-performing companies do to prepare for and implement change are reviewed and the characteristics of the most effective change managers are also discussed. Tools you can use to assess the level of change readiness in others and techniques to move people to the next level are provided.

Chapter Seven, "Bridge Builder 6: Increase Coordination and Collaboration," explains why we would rather compete than collaborate and what you can do to create a climate in which people are motivated to cooperate and work effectively together. You'll find specific techniques that will help you increase the likelihood that people will work effectively together, within teams and across organizational boundaries, to achieve department and business unit objectives.

I hope you will find this book helpful as you navigate the ups and downs of our turbulent economy. The good news is that the tips and techniques it contains are research-based, grounded in logic, and easy to follow.

Effective execution is about the consistent application of practical common-sense actions—it's not "glamorous" or "sexy." It was my goal to write a book filled with practical, nitty-gritty, nose-to-the-grindstone advice you can start using right away. I hope I got it done. And once you've put the content into practice inside your organization, I hope you'll be able to say the same.

Closing the Execution Gap

Chapter One

Vision Without Execution
Is Hallucination

Once upon a time, not so many years ago, strategy was king. Leaders immersed themselves in the matter of planning how best to achieve their company's goals. The subject of strategy dominated the attention of senior executives and the writings of consultants and management gurus. Experts of various stripes weighed in on how to put strategic planning processes in place and transform employees at all levels into strategic thinkers.

Naturally, leaders assumed all this strategizing would pay off. And yet, for too many organizations the results promised to flow from these well-crafted visions went unrealized.

Quite simply, they couldn't *execute*.

> Now, strategy's hey-day has passed. The business world has shifted its focus to execution — execution of plans and initiatives and the consistent delivery of results. If an organization can't execute, nothing else matters: not the most solid, well-thought-out strategy, not the most innovative business model, not even the invention of technology that could transform an industry.

Thomas Edison famously said: "Vision without execution is hallucination." It's true. And as the hallucinations of countless business leaders have proved, knowing what you want to do or where you want the company to be in three to five years may be less than half the battle.

So what's the problem? Why—given all the buzz about having a clear and compelling vision and a realistic and feasible strategy—can't some leaders seem to execute?

This is a question I pondered for a very long time. My work with senior teams made me curious about why, despite having a sound strategic planning process in place and teams made up of smart, experienced professionals, many organizations still struggled and were unable to get things done and deliver results.

It seemed obvious there was a gap between planning and execution. And while much had been written on the need for leaders to improve their ability to execute, I could find very little information on what causes this gap and why it exists in some organizations but not in others. In addition, specific guidelines for solving this problem were even more elusive.

So my company, Onpoint Consulting, set out to gather specific information on what it takes to effectively execute plans and initiatives. We designed a study to answer three questions:

- Is there a gap between an organization's ability to formulate a vision and strategy and achieve business results?
- What differentiates organizations that are more effective at execution from those that are less effective?
- What can leaders do to enhance their organization's ability to close the strategy-execution gap and achieve business results?

We asked leaders in the pharmaceuticals, chemical, healthcare, insurance, financial services, and manufacturing industries to complete an online survey designed around these three questions. Response choices ranged from 5 = *Strongly Agree* to 1 = *Strongly Disagree*, and a "Don't Know" option was also provided.

In addition, we asked leaders whether they believe there is a gap between the ability of their companies to develop and communicate a sound strategy and implement the strategy successfully. Participating companies had more than one hundred employees and more than $10M in revenue. A total of 409 middle- and senior-level leaders responded.

As part of our analysis—a very important part—we looked at the differences between the most-successful and least-successful companies. We asked respondents to indicate the extent to which sales, revenue, and net earnings had increased or decreased over the last three years. We used a performance composite score based on net sales and net earnings to identify the most successful companies (see the Appendix).

The chapter you're reading is all about what we learned.

Yes, There Is an Execution Gap—But That's Only the Tip of the Iceberg!

We expected some percentage of leaders to report a gap between their organization's ability to formulate and communicate a vision and strategy and its ability to deliver results. Anecdotal evidence suggested that the number was fairly substantial. And our suspicions were confirmed: nearly half of the 409 leaders we surveyed (49 percent) believed there was a strategy-execution gap in their organizations.

Here's what really surprised us: only 36 percent of leaders responded positively to the question, "I have confidence in my organization's ability to close the gap between strategy and execution." Said another way, a staggering 64 percent of leaders who indicated there was a strategy-execution gap lack confidence that it can be closed.

To provide further insight, we segmented survey respondents into four categories (see Figure 1.1).

- *True Believers:* Those who believe that their organizations are executing effectively and are not struggling with a strategy-execution gap

Figure 1.1 Doubters, Optimists, and True Believers

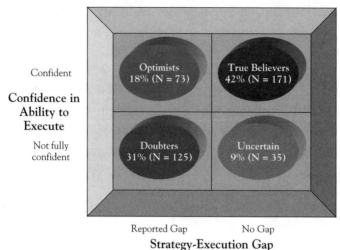

Strategy-Execution Gap

- *Doubters:* Those who reported a gap and lack confidence it can be closed
- *Optimists:* Those who reported a gap, but are confident that the gap can be closed
- *Uncertain:* Those who did not report a strategy-execution gap but who did indicate that they lack confidence in their organizations' ability to effectively execute

We found that only 42 percent of those who participated in the study were "True Believers." This finding—coupled with the high percentage of leaders who don't believe their organizations can close the gap—underscores the magnitude of the strategy-execution problem.

If people's perceptions of their company can be trusted—and it stands to reason that the men and women responsible for getting things done day to day have the clearest viewpoint of all—this confidence problem is troubling. It suggests that most organizations simply aren't set up to execute well.

Right now you may be thinking, "Okay, I know my organization suffers from an execution problem. I've known for some time. But what can we do about it? What's the secret to ensuring effective execution—and consequently, gaining people's confidence that the organization is capable of achieving its intended business results?"

"Conventional Wisdom": Maybe Not So Wise!

If you're like many leaders, you've bought into the conventional wisdom about strategy execution. It goes something like this: communicate an inspiring vision and realistic strategies, make sure you have an engaged and committed workforce with the skills to do the job, provide high-quality products and services, and focus on the customer to ensure success. Admittedly, it sounds good. But all evidence indicates that something is missing from the equation.

It's true that these baseline practices are necessary and relevant. Unfortunately, they are *not* sufficient to ensure successful implementation. Most of the organizations in our study—those afflicted with a strategy-execution gap and those who are not—have these practices in place. In fact, the five items contained in the "conventional wisdom" statement above and shown in Figure 1.2 were among the highest-rated in our study. Plus, these factors are also reported to be in place in top-performing and less-successful companies alike.

Here are some of the things we learned from our study regarding "conventional wisdom":

Companies Have "Vision" and "Strategy" in Abundance

As the baseline practices show, organizations reporting a strategy-execution gap don't trace the issue back to an unclear vision or an unrealistic business strategy. In fact, despite the high percentage

Figure 1.2 Top Five Items

	Favorable	Neutral	Unfavorable
People in my work unit are committed to doing what is required to help the company succeed.	84%	12%	4%
People in my work unit have the skills and experience needed to do their jobs effectively.	82%	12%	6%
My company's strategy is realistic.	79%	13%	8%
My company maintains a high level of quality and customer service.	77%	16%	8%
My company has a clear and inspiring vision for the future.	75%	12%	13%

A five-point rating scale was used:
5 = Strongly Agree, 4 = Agree, 3 = Neither Agree nor Disagree, 2 = Disagree, 1 = Strongly Disagree
Ratings of "4" or "5" are considered favorable, ratings of "3" neutral, and ratings of "1" or "2" unfavorable.

of leaders our study turned up who perceive there is an execution gap, a large majority of respondents believe their companies have clear and inspiring visions (75 percent) and realistic strategies (79 percent).

Of the leaders reporting a gap, 63 percent believe their companies' visions are clear and inspiring, and 69 percent believe their strategies are realistic. Even in less-successful companies, a high percentage of respondents believe the visions are clear and inspiring (56 percent) and the strategies are realistic (67 percent).

Few would argue that a clear, inspiring vision and a realistic strategy are fundamental for business success. (That they are central to success is supported by the fact that respondents in top-performing companies provided significantly higher ratings on these items.) However, our study indicates that effective execution and performance results are not *guaranteed* by having these factors in place. Crafting a realistic, inspiring vision and gaining employee buy-in is clearly just a first step.

Lack of Employee Commitment Isn't the Problem, Either

It's widely believed that employee commitment is a critical component of an organization's ability to execute effectively. And it does make sense: employees who care will naturally exert more effort to get the job done than employees who don't. Although our results do support this premise, we found commitment not to be a differentiator. *All* organizations—those with gaps and those without, the successful and the not-so-successful—report that they are staffed by committed employees.

We used two questions to measure commitment: "People in my work unit are committed to doing what is required to help the company succeed" and (to measure discretionary effort) "People in my work unit look for new and better ways of doing things."

The former question is one of the five highest-rated items in our survey: even among those who reported strategy-execution gaps, 79 percent provided favorable ratings. The latter was one of the ten highest-rated items, and 70 percent of people reporting gaps provided favorable ratings. The upshot is that these items did not differentiate the "Gap" from the "No Gap" companies, nor did they differentiate the top-performers from their less-successful counterparts.

We Found No Shortage of Skills

Obviously, in order to execute well, people must have the skills and experience needed to perform their jobs. And evidently, most do. Our results indicate that all organizations—those that execute well, those that are struggling with a gap, the top performers, and the less-successful—have this factor in place. Not only was "skills and experience" one of the top five highest-rated items in our survey, but among those who reported a strategy-execution gap, 76 percent gave it a favorable score. Like commitment, while it is a prerequisite for success, it doesn't appear to be a differentiator.

The Customer Isn't Being Neglected

Our study also revealed that the strategy-execution gap is likely *not* related to shoddy quality or second-rate customer service. Despite the high percentage of leaders reporting a gap, this item was rated among the top five, with 77 percent of leaders providing favorable ratings overall. And even among leaders who reported gaps, 65 percent gave this item high marks.

So here's the question: If these five factors—a clear and inspiring vision, a realistic strategy, employee commitment, a workforce with the skills to do their jobs, and high levels of quality and customer service—are prerequisites for successful execution, what is it that puts organizations over the top? What sets the best apart from the rest?

The Five Bridges: Gap-Closers That Make the Difference

First, take a look at Figures 1.3 and 1.4. You'll see that five factors set apart the organizations with the best performance results *and* the companies more effective at execution. That is, they

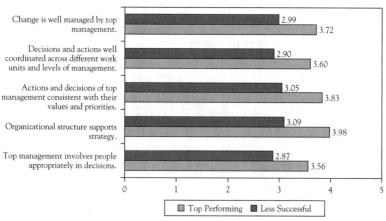

Figure 1.3 Good Versus Great

	Top Performing	Less Successful
Change is well managed by top management.	2.99	3.72
Decisions and actions well coordinated across different work units and levels of management.	2.90	3.60
Actions and decisions of top management consistent with their values and priorities.	3.05	3.83
Organizational structure supports strategy.	3.09	3.98
Top management involves people appropriately in decisions.	2.87	3.56

A five-point rating scale was used:
5 = Strongly Agree, 4 = Agree, 3 = Neither Agree nor Disagree, 2 = Disagree, 1 = Strongly Disagree
All reported differences are significant at the p<.05 level.

Figure 1.4 No Gap Versus Gap

Change is well managed by top management. — 2.84 / 3.83

Decisions and actions well coordinated across different work units and levels of management. — 2.79 / 3.79

Actions and decisions of top management consistent with their values and priorities. — 2.99 / 3.97

Organizational structure supports strategy. — 3.08 / 4.11

Top management involves people appropriately in decisions. — 2.68 / 3.76

□ No Gap ■ Gap

A five-point rating scale was used:
5 = Strongly Agree, 4 = Agree, 3 = Neither Agree nor Disagree, 2 = Disagree, 1 = Strongly Disagree
All reported differences are significant at the p<.05 level.

differentiated the "No Gaps" from the "Gaps." And this is interesting: in companies whose leaders *did* report gaps, the presence of these factors contributed to confidence that the gap could be closed (Figure 1.5).

I think of these differentiating factors as "The Five Bridges." If you have them in place in your company, you are more likely to be able to keep the strategy execution gap from forming to begin with, or close the gap once it has formed.

One important disclaimer: these bridges are not permanent. Once you've built them, you must keep vigilant watch over them and work hard to maintain them over time. It's quite possible for a company to have a bridge in place one year, only to discover that over time it's weakened or even crumbled and is no longer able to help your people traverse the gap.

As we get further into the book, we'll discuss specific actions—meant to be taken at the individual manager level—that will help you and your company construct these bridges. For now, though, I'd like to touch on what the bridges look like in action—and what the absence of them looks like as well.

Figure 1.5 What Separates Optimists from Doubters

	Optimists	Doubters
Change is well managed by top management.	3.54	2.43
Decisions and actions well coordinated across different work units and levels of management.	3.37	2.46
Actions and decisions of top management consistent with their values and priorities.	3.64	2.62
Organizational structure supports strategy.	3.67	2.74
Top management involves people appropriately in decisions.	3.29	2.34

A five-point rating scale was used:
5 = Strongly Agree, 4 = Agree, 3 = Neither Agree nor Disagree, 2 = Disagree, 1 = Strongly Disagree
All reported differences are significant at the p<.05 level.

To that end, let's take a quick look at some real-world companies that execute well (we'll call them the Gap Closers) and those who don't (we'll call them the Gap Makers).

Bridge 1: The Ability to Manage Change

We all know change is inevitable. However, despite their sincerest efforts, many companies can't seem to operationalize that knowledge and turn it into positive action. And that's a dangerous shortcoming. Embracing the spirit of innovation and change can help you reach new levels of success, while being rigid and unwilling to change can cause serious, perhaps irreparable, harm.

> Make no mistake: if you want to run a successful business, you have to be willing to create and implement innovative strategies and adjust to changes in the market. That's true of small businesses and huge,

international corporations alike. If you're not flexible enough to bend with the winds of change like a palm tree or a bamboo, you'll snap in half like a Bradford pear when the first storm comes along.

A Gap Closer: Procter & Gamble. A few years back, P&G hit a home run with its Mr. Clean Magic Eraser. It was, without a doubt, a fantastic product. But what makes it relevant to Bridge 1 lies in how the product came to fruition. The organization, which embraced CEO Alan G. Lafley's "customer is king" philosophy, had a track record of focusing on their needs and developing new products for them in house. With the Magic Eraser, it broke from that model.

A P&G employee actually discovered the prototype in Japan. And rather than limiting itself to internal ideas, Procter & Gamble saw an opportunity to license a product that already existed and tap into its organizational competence to add value. Its plan to use ideas that have been developed outside the company worked due to P&G's openness to change and its ability to execute flawlessly. The Magic Eraser and Procter & Gamble's similar products have made it a success story year after year.

A Gap Maker: Dell. Just as people can get stuck in a rut, so can businesses. Dell developed "The Dell Way," and the company's reluctance to tread off of the beaten path cost it its customers. In the early 2000s, the company was able to attract customers to its website with low-cost offers that required the buyer to make additions in order to have the best computer (which, of course, meant the price would end up being more than the original low-cost offer). By 2006, however, consumers didn't have to go to Dell to get a "custom-made" computer. Why? Because there were tons of affordable computers out there with all of the bells and whistles that consumers wanted.

Here's where Dell turned a problem into a *huge* problem. When its leaders realized they were losing business to competitors, they fell back on a practice that had always worked for them before: they cut costs to maintain market share. One area that suffered was customer service, which had originally been one of the company's biggest strengths. Basically, Dell created a customer service nightmare. The company has recently made changes to get back on course, but once you've lost consumer confidence, it can be hard to get it back.

Bridge 2: A Structure That Supports Execution

Our research found that striking the right balance between centralization and decentralization differentiates top-performing companies from less-successful ones. Many organizations place great emphasis on developing an exciting vision and a realistic strategy and engaging employees. That's all well and good... but the problem comes when leaders assume the current organizational structure and systems will support the new strategy. Sometimes it's just not true.

And don't assume that organizational structure is just about efficiency. The right structure can also enhance accountability, coordination, and communication and ensure that decisions are being made as close to the action as possible. These are key components to getting things done.

A Gap Closer: Hewlett-Packard. When Mark Hurd became CEO of Hewlett-Packard, he was constantly being asked if he thought acquiring Compaq was a good idea. His answer? The question is irrelevant. Basically, Hurd said what's done is done, and his job now was to find a way to make it work. He did just that when he reorganized the company into three divisions, with each division having its own sales force, making the heads of the divisions responsible for sales. He also reorganized the IT function. Instead of having eighty-five data centers, he centralized them into three.

Essentially, Hurd decentralized the sales force and centralized the IT function of the company. This is the opposite of the way the company was organized before, and it ensured the organizational structure would be better aligned with the business strategy. One measure of HP's success is that operating profit increased during 2006 by 31 percent.

Another Gap Closer: IBM. In 2007, IBM set out to become a "globally integrated enterprise." The key? It put in place a structure that best supports this strategy. Historically, IBM created mini versions of itself in each country where it operated. As it turned out, this was inefficient and expensive. Now the company sets up shop wherever it finds the right talent at the right price: for example, global IT service delivery in India, global supply chain in China, and a global financing back office in Brazil. IBM also redesigned business processes and automated work with software to help coordinate these activities.

In addition, to keep the supply of human capital flowing to wherever it is needed, HR shifted from a silo structure to three cross-functional teams, each dedicated to a specific set of employees. The change worked: In the second quarter of 2007, IBM's revenues increased 9 percent to $23.8 billion, and each division reported healthy growth. And they continue to do well. Revenue and net income grew from $91.4 billion and $9.4 billion respectively in 2007 to $103.6 billion and $12.3 billion in 2009.

A Gap Maker: Wal-Mart (Seiyu Stores). Since first investing in Seiyu Stores in 2002 and eventually taking full control, Wal-Mart has reportedly never managed to make the stores profitable. In 2008 the company had a net loss of 25.8 billion yen, which is about US$284,000,000, primarily due to the closure of unprofitable stores. Several decisions made by the retail giant have created employee distrust and consumer apathy: laying off employees, cutting out distribution middlemen, mandating that stores stay open twenty-four hours, and introducing low-cost products that don't meet Japanese tastes or standards of quality.

Many observers attribute these problems to the fact that Wal-Mart's international operations are centrally controlled in the United States by people who lack appropriate international experience and knowledge of the intricate aspects of Japanese culture. In addition, Wal-Mart's and Seiyu's systems have not meshed well, resulting in many products not being ordered on time and suppliers not being paid on time.

Bridge 3: Employee Involvement in Decision Making

> Involving employees in decision making is controversial. Some leaders view it as a sign of weakness. Others fear giving up control. In reality, though, the world is too complex for any leader to go it alone. To make good decisions, you must seek out the perspectives of a wide range of people. Involving people in decisions gets them focused on generating solutions to problems rather than complaining or waiting to be told what to do.

Your employees shouldn't feel like they exist only to help your company make huge profits. They need to feel respected as key players with valid viewpoints. They should be involved in all critical decisions that affect them and should be allowed—even encouraged—to freely share their thoughts and concerns.

If your employees don't have a sense of ownership, nothing truly great can occur. You must build employee involvement and engagement into your company's culture. Don't merely welcome their ideas; actively solicit them.

A Gap Closer: Costco. The big box retailer headquartered in Seattle, Washington, is consistently on our list of companies that are among the best at execution and getting things done.

Why? A big part of its success comes down to the fact that Costco treats its store managers like entrepreneurs. They are allowed to make decisions and choices that meet the needs of the shoppers in their geographies.

Of course, these entrepreneurial managers don't make decisions in a vacuum. They do so within the parameters set by the company. Costco has a remarkable ability to simultaneously focus on two performance areas that appear to be mutually exclusive: cost containment and growth. It is obsessive about keeping costs low. It does not use pricey ad agencies. There are no commissioned salespeople. Signage looks like it came off a laser printer. And yes, there are no shopping bags. Yet, with $72.48 billion in sales as of 2008, Costco has never had a negative monthly same-store sales result (excluding the impact of the strong dollar and lower gas prices in fiscal year 2008) since it was founded twenty-three years ago.

Another Gap Closer: Google. When Google started out, it was easy to keep all of their employees involved—primarily because there were so few of them. But now that the company has expanded to thousands of employees, leaders have had to find ways to ensure that everyone has a voice. One way they keep their ears open to grassroots ideas is by allowing engineers to spend at least one day a week working on their own pet projects. The company also uses smaller teams to develop new concepts—sometimes assigning only three or four people to a team.

Now, compare Google's approach to employee involvement and engagement to another computer-centric company: Microsoft. One reason Microsoft has run into problems in the past was its tendency to have many large teams working on the same project. The lack of communication and coordination between teams can lead to problems. For example, when Microsoft was developing its new operating system, one team placed a set of icons on the right while another placed the same set of icons on the left. Google avoids these problems by using small teams. Members of a small team have more ownership and accountability and can more easily communicate and execute their ideas.

A Gap Maker: The NBA. When the National Basketball Association (NBA) tried to introduce a new basketball, guess who they forgot to involve in the decision: *the players.* That's right. The NBA came up with a new ball design and never once asked the players how they liked it while it was in development. There's no reasonable explanation for this faux pas. Asking the players would have increased the quality of the ball itself *and* the acceptance of the new ball decision.

Instead, the NBA ended up with a ball that players refused to use because they felt it was difficult to handle when it was damp and it would actually cut their fingers. Because of the player backlash, the NBA had to scrap it's "improved" model and go back to the ball the players preferred—the one they have been using for decades. This anecdote is a glaring example of why it is important to involve people whose support you need to execute decisions that affect them.

Another Gap Maker: Merrill Lynch. Another cautionary tale on not involving people in decisions comes out of Merrill Lynch just before it was acquired by Bank of America. Many observers saw its breakdown in risk management as a matter of poor execution. Although Stanley O'Neal has been credited with boosting Merrill's profitability and transforming it into an international firm, former employees point to a flaw in his leadership style. He is said to be uncomfortable around people with views different from his own, and some report that he did not engage in debate with individuals who could have helped him steer clear of the sub-prime troubles. As a result, when the market value of Merrill's asset-backed debt fell, the information may not have moved through the corporate hierarchy, which made it difficult for the firm to respond quickly.

Bridge 4: Alignment Between Leader Actions and Company Values and Priorities

No company should ever have two sets of values and expectations: one for the leader(s) and one for the employees. For one thing, it's not fair. But that's not even the real issue. The real issue is that when leaders say one thing and do another, business suffers. Of course, we all know that leader behavior is relevant. Still, it might surprise you to learn exactly how much execution depends on how consistent the leader's behavior is with organizational values and priorities.

> One, people watch the leader for signals about what is important and appropriate. They pattern their behavior after yours. Two, if your behavior signifies that "we are all in this together," people are more likely to be motivated and go the proverbial extra mile. When you expect employees to behave a certain way (such as better serving the customer or minimizing waste) or ask employees to focus on certain priorities (like cost containment or innovation), you'd better do the same. A do-as-I-say, not-as-I-do attitude sends mixed messages and breeds resentment.

The behaviors and priorities that pertain to employees must also pertain to leaders. If employees at your company start asking: "Why is it necessary for us but not for them?" don't be surprised when they resist needed change—or when performance falls short of expectations.

A Gap Closer: Costco (Yes, Again!). James D. Sinegal, president and CEO of Costco, is one of the best and most consistent examples of a leader whose behavior is aligned with the organization's values and priorities. Costco will not mark an item up more than 14 percent, unlike supermarkets and departments stores that mark up merchandise 25 to 50 percent. Low markups may generate sales but they also mean lower profits and Costco's pretax margins are around 3 percent. Yet, despite the microscopic margins, the company earned $1.28 billion in 2008 through its membership fee and its Spartan approach to costs. The fact that the CEO "walks the talk" is at least partially responsible for Costco's success.

In an environment of razor-thin margins, store managers need to be obsessively focused on details. Sinegal models that behavior every time he visits a warehouse store. He quizzes store managers about the sales of each department, what they are doing to move merchandise, and the progress of individual items. Here's another way Sinegal signals the importance of keeping costs low: his office overlooks the parking lot of the Costco across the street and he has folding chairs for visitors. He answers his own phone and does not have an entourage like many successful senior executives. His salary and bonus total about $450,000. Now there is someone who lives the values and keeps the organization's priorities front and center every day.

A Gap Maker: AMR Corp. The story of Donald Carty, former president of American Airlines, illustrates the importance of a leader modeling the attitudes and behaviors he or she expects of employees. In 2003, shortly after getting employees to take significant pay and benefits cuts, he offered gigantic "stay bonuses" to the members of his senior management team. Carty lost total credibility with his company and had to step down. You would think that the executives at AMR, the parent company of American Airlines, would have learned the lessons of not "walking the talk"—but clearly that is not the case.

In 2007 the top five officers of AMR Corp. shared a compensation package worth about $16.5 million that year and the chief executive, Gerard Arpey, received a package worth about $6.6 million. In 2009 management bonuses once again angered union members as CEO Arpey again awarded himself a bonus ($225,000, down from $1.7 million the year before). Although this seems modest enough, the pilots' union estimates that American management has received more than $296 million in bonuses since 1996, while 27,000 jobs have been lost.

More Gap Makers: TARP Bailout-Seeking Auto Executives. In 2008 the CEOs of General Motors, Ford, and Chrysler shocked members of the U.S. Congress, and the American people, when they used private jets to travel to Washington, D.C., for a hearing. What made it so shocking was that the CEOs were going to Washington to ask for government assistance to help their companies get through the worst recession in U.S. history and the worst market for car sales in the history of the automotive industry. As several Congressmen pointed out, behavior so inconsistent with what was being described as a crisis is an example of how the automotive executives helped create the problem they now find themselves in and how unaware they are about the connection between their behavior and the current situation.

Bridge 5: Company-Wide Coordination and Cooperation

I think we can all agree: most employees approach their work with good intentions. They want to cooperate with colleagues and co-workers. Few people will consciously sabotage their own livelihood. Yet, ensuring that decisions and actions are coordinated across organizational boundaries requires more than faith and words alone. It takes shared goals and clearly defined roles; these provide the foundation upon which cooperation and coordination can be built.

In addition, people must be held accountable—for fulfilling commitments, meeting obligations and taking responsibility for doing their jobs properly. This requires a combination of direct leader behavior and systems that encourage and reinforce the appropriate behavior among employees.

A Gap Closer: Cisco Systems. Since 2001 Cisco, led by John Chambers, has been on a journey to enhance its ability to execute plans and get things done day-to-day. Its first step? Reorganizing the company around functions. Whenever they wanted to enter a new market or geography, business unit leaders brought together team members from these functional groups. To help ensure cross-organizational cooperation, Chambers changed the compensation system so that people were paid not only for hitting their targets, but also on how effectively they collaborated with their peers.

Technology has also played an important role in facilitating teamwork. Cisco has installed 120 telepresence centers (a new high-end video conferencing system) across the company and uses social networking to bring together employees from around the world. By all measures the company has been very successful—in 2007 sales increased 23 percent to $35 billion, profits climbed 31 percent to $7.3 billion, and revenue rose 17 percent, not including acquisitions. Cisco continued to demonstrate strong performance in 2008 despite a dramatically depressed global economy. Revenue of $39.5 billion, an 11 percent increase from 2007, and net income of $8.0 billion, an increase of 8 percent from 2007, shows the impact excellent execution can have on overall business performance—even in an economy that is shrinking or growing very slowly.

A Gap Maker: Toyota. In 2010, many people were surprised when Toyota, a brand known for its quality and reliability, recalled over six million cars due to a faulty accelerator pedal. How did this once mighty brand end up with such a PR disaster on its hands?

Toyota used to work with one supplier for each part. But when a fire at a supplier's facility caused twenty plants to shut down for five days, Toyota decided it needed a second source as a back-up. For the accelerator, however, the company failed to ensure the parts it was receiving from the two suppliers were identical.

Analysts attribute the lack of communication and coordination that led to the parts mishap to a bureaucracy that could not accommodate the company's rapid growth and to a focus on profit that led executives to ignore principles that had contributed to its previously untarnished reputation. But the Toyota breakdown isn't only about this one bridge. It also illustrates how fragile *each* of the five bridges is and why they require constant vigilance—having a bridge in place one year doesn't mean it will always remain strong and help people traverse the gap.

One More Gap Maker: The Federal Aviation Administration (FAA). If you've flown recently, you've experienced another example of poor coordination and cooperation. Despite the efforts of the Federal Aviation Administration (FAA), air travel is worse than ever. More than 909,000 flights were late through June of 2007 (twice the level of 2002), and almost everyone has a horror story involving missed connections, lost luggage, or hours spent waiting on the tarmac.

The obstacle to finding a solution does not seem to be either of the usual suspects, funding shortfalls (the FAA did not spend all the money it was allocated in 2006) or lack of know-how (existing technology could meet the demand created by the increased number of fliers). Instead, it appears the FAA is unable to break the gridlock among the key players in the system. Big airlines, small aircraft owners, labor unions, politicians, airplane manufacturers, and other parties fight to protect their interests and blame each other for causing the problems.

So yes, these Five Execution Bridges are critical. If they aren't in place, you will have a tough time achieving your company's goals. The more bridges you have in place, the more likely you are to reach your goals—and the lack of any one of them could potentially derail your efforts.

Figure 1.6 Bottom Five Items

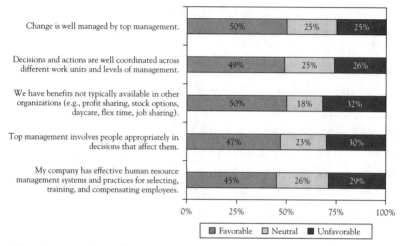

A five-point rating scale was used:
5 = Strongly Agree, 4 = Agree, 3 = Neither Agree nor Disagree, 2 = Disagree, 1 = Strongly Disagree
Ratings of "4" or "5" are considered favorable, ratings of "3" neutral, and ratings of "1" or "2" unfavorable.

It's clear that many organizations struggle with building these bridges. In fact, three of them were among the lowest-rated in our study, as shown in Figure 1.6. Either decision-makers are complacent because they're following what conventional wisdom dictates and assume that's enough, or they believe that changing what's wrong is outside their purview.

The Bottom Line

Today, most leaders understand that a well-thought-out and energizing vision and a realistic strategy are critical to success. They appreciate the need for highly engaged employees with the skills required to do the job, for high-quality products and services, and for listening to the customer. Yet, even when these core factors are in place, many organizations are still not able to deliver consistent results. Although essential, these factors are clearly only prerequisites.

Companies and managers who are the best at execution also create operational plans that are coordinated across departments and levels, expect and encourage top performance from everyone, hold people accountable for results and create a culture of responsibility, make high quality decisions by ensuring the right people are talking about the right things at the right time, and facilitate individual change readiness.

If other companies can build and maintain the bridges that close the execution gap, so can yours. The rest of the book will help you accomplish this. I will discuss six specific actions—to continue my analogy I'll call them Bridge Builders—that leaders at any level of the organization can immediately put into practice. Of course, you won't bridge the execution gap overnight, and once built, the bridges won't be self-sustaining. Still, getting this "construction project" underway is a step in the right direction.

Chapter Two

Bridge Builder 1: Translate Strategy into Action

Action plans are the cornerstone of execution. Still, there was a time when I was hesitant to discuss action planning with managers and senior executives because I worried that I would be stating the obvious. Eventually, though, I realized that few people were consistently creating and using action plans.

Naturally, there is always an explanation: *Things move too fast and I don't have time for planning,* for instance, or *Things change too frequently to make the plan useful.* The irony is that these excuses actually make the case for action planning.

Complex initiatives require plans to monitor progress and ensure that deliverables are produced on time and on budget. And the frantic pace and frequent changes that define the 21st century workday make action planning even more essential. Without a base plan in place, how will you know what adjustments need to be made when things change? How else can you keep track of multiple deadlines and accountabilities in a fast-paced environment?

> A well-thought-out action plan is one of the best tools you have to ensure that the factors required for effective execution are in place. It is a catalyst for ongoing conversations between stakeholders. It also provides the context for the effective use of the Bridge Builders

and a variety of related actions: setting expectations, clarifying accountability, identifying who needs to be involved in decisions, managing changes in project scope and timing, highlighting where coordination and cooperation are required, establishing priorities, allocating resources, and keeping commitments to a reasonable level.

Of course, some organizations do develop and use action plans. But based on my work with clients I find it startling how many of them treat the action plan as an obligatory administrative device rather than a useful tool to help manage the business. In these cases, people fail to make an explicit connection between their action plans and their business strategies.

Action plans are the way you translate broad strategic objectives into specific, more easily monitored activities for teams and individuals. In addition to helping to manage the work, action plans help bridge the gap between business strategy and results. Figure 2.1 depicts the strategic management process and shows where action plans come in—and how they connect strategy and results.

First Things First: A Brief Look at Strategic Planning

Although a detailed discussion of the strategic planning process is beyond the scope of this book, I'd like to spend a little time on two outputs of the process: clarity about the current strategic state of your business and its vision for the future. Both have implications for the plans you develop and how you execute those plans. Of course, there are dozens of approaches to developing a business strategy. The list below provides a brief overview of the strategic planning process I commonly use with senior teams.

Figure 2.1 The Strategic Management Process

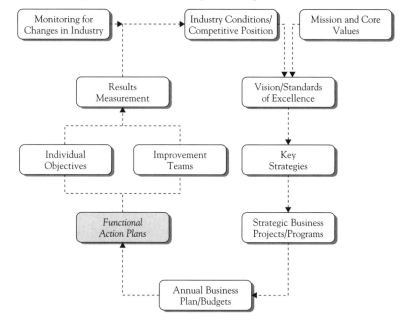

Strategic Planning Process

- Define the industry and business.
- Analyze the industry's attractiveness and its potential for growth and profitability (Opportunities and Threats).
- Analyze the current competitive position of industry participants (Strengths and Weaknesses).
- List key assumptions that have driven the analysis.
- Identify the current Strategic State and options for business strategies, and develop alternatives and contingencies.
- Develop a Mission and a Vision of the future state of the business.
- Commit to pursue a future Strategic State and business strategies.

- Generate options for strategic projects and programs.
- Analyze the costs and benefits of each alternative and decide which to implement.
- Plan for implementation.
- Revisit and revise the plan often.

From Soaring to Circling: The Strategic States Model

The Strategic States Model describes four natural strategic directions an organization can take in order to respond positively to conditions in its environment: *Eagle, Fort, Slim Down,* and *Circled Wagons.*[1] Every business entity—whether it's a corporation, a business, or a function—faces conditions that indicate one of these four states. Each state requires a unique focus and set of behaviors for effective execution.

The Strategic States Model is based on four assumptions:

- Any strategy adopted by any organization will fall into one of the four strategic state categories.
- Any strategic state chosen implies the deliberate use of a certain set of business strategies and suggests that others may be difficult or unwise to implement.
- Implementation plans, management systems, and organizational culture should all support the strategic state, keeping in mind that each state has a range of requirements and downsides that must also be attended to.
- The strategic state shifts over time as the organization acts and responds to conditions in the environment.

Your company's strategic state determines what you need to attend to in order to ensure effective execution. Why have I included it as a prelude to the "vision" section? Because you need to know where you are (and why) before you can know where you are going. Getting a handle on your current strategic state—that is, your organization's capability relative to its competitors; its strengths and weaknesses—is the first step in developing a feasible and realistic vision of where the company needs to be in three or five years.

Following are brief descriptions of each of the four strategic states and what effective execution in each state requires:

The Eagle State. Eagle strategies are used to manage the creation of a new business, product, or market. It's easy to see how this strategic state gets its name. Eagles are keen-sighted, strong, and fearless; they attack prey that can be overwhelmed swiftly and without warning. Like its avian counterpart, the business in an Eagle Strategic State is looking for prey—new opportunities or ones that have previously gone unnoticed. Forward integration, creation of excess capacity to meet future growth, the development of a new foreign business—all are Eagle strategies.

Businesses in the Eagle Strategic State must be prepared to deal with unknowns, accept high risk, and focus on targets that are vulnerable to their unique advantages. Eagle businesses may be parts of larger, more established corporations or they may be fledgling companies. Internet start-ups like Skype, a voice over Internet protocol (VoIP) provider and Central Desktop, a provider of online project collaboration software, are Eagle ventures. They are, to paraphrase the announcer's comments at the start of "Star Trek," boldly going where no man or woman has gone before.

Effective execution in the Eagle State requires the ability to:

- Apply outstanding marketing skills and sustain aggressive marketing efforts
- Sustain management dedication and commitment

- Finance high-growth and high-risk ventures
- Manage highly leveraged conditions
- Pursue fast growth
- Innovate rapidly from the original concept to propel growth
- Recognize signs of maturation and alter the strategic direction accordingly
- Develop and maintain an innovative or unique technological advantage

The Fort State. An Eagle establishes its nest in defensible areas and increases the nest size year after year. Businesses do the same. As a company becomes strong and well-established, it moves into the Fort Strategic State. The word "fort" comes from the Sanskrit word meaning "to strengthen or elevate." Companies that follow this strategy do exactly that. They strengthen an existing organization and continue to elevate the market position of their products and services over those of their competitors.

A wide variety of business strategies may be used to maintain a Fort Strategic State. The most dramatic and highest-risk strategy for a Fort is market penetration: the attack on another Fort. The market war between Coca-Cola and Pepsi for leadership in the soft drink industry or Microsoft and Google for dominance in Internet search is a prime example. Forts also pursue strategies designed to maintain market share position, grow with industry volume, and achieve operational excellence. While these strategies may result in occasional attacks on their positions, they do not require the war-like mentality of the market penetration strategy. Forts may also choose to solidify their positions through emphasis on technological breakthroughs in process capabilities.

All Fort strategies involve active efforts to maintain, improve, and strengthen market position. However, companies that embrace these Fort strategies must understand the dangers of becoming a "cash cow." Too many strong businesses have been milked to death by complacency and by the assumption that they will stay on top of the industry by simply doing what they have done in the past.

For effective execution the Fort State requires:

- Outstanding technology, production, and marketing skills
- A highly structured and professionally managed entity
- An outstanding competitive intelligence system
- Clear policies and procedures that facilitate opera-tions in a large, complex organization
- Exceptional performance standards for all functions and employees
- Clear reward systems
- Aggressive dedication to market position and the capacity to respond to any attack

The Slim-Down State. Ideally, Eagles become Forts, then spin off more Eagles. But not every business achieves this cycle. Without an emphasis on continuous improvement a Fort can become fat. Due to a changing environment, past decisions that determined appropriate product lines, market segments, and organizational structure may no longer benefit the current business. Or perhaps the growth of the existing organization has slowed or stopped, but the Fort systems and structures survive.

When a business overextends itself and current conditions no longer provide adequate returns, it's time for a Slim-Down Strategic State. The business needs to go on a diet. The diet analogy is appropriate in several ways. First, when people develop good habits, monitor their food intake, and adjust it to changes in lifestyle, dieting never becomes necessary. Likewise, a business that has made a habit of adjusting to its environment should never have to go into a prolonged Slim-Down Strategic State.

If any of these factors slip (and they apparently often do), it's important for both people and businesses to recognize the need to slim down, do it as healthily as possible, and move on—hopefully retaining those better habits.

Finally, just as a diet can be detrimental if taken to extremes, the health of a business can be compromised if the Slim-Down is taken too far for too long. Long-term "slimming down" can lead to debilitating concessions to the competition and irreversible damage to the organization.

The need for a Slim-Down is often the result of external factors that are not within the full control of business. Still, whatever the cause, a quick response is needed in order to avoid dire consequences. A company in the Slim-Down Strategic State might choose to pursue such business strategies as product line, production, distribution, or market rationalization, or stripping the business down to the most profitable piece. Management must plan carefully for the restructuring of plants, markets, and products and accurately assess the value and viability of the reduced configuration. When strategies are not identified early and made a conscious, common goal, the Slim-Down Strategic State can become extended and debilitating.

For effective execution the Slim-Down State requires:

- Focus on the planned restructuring of plants, markets, and products

- Accurate evaluation of the value and viability of the new reduced configuration

The Circled Wagons State. In the life of a business, events or conditions may arise that are so ominous they require the suspension of the current strategy until the environment changes. Like pioneers who positioned their wagons in a protective circle, the business positions itself defensively with the sole purpose of surviving an attack of life-threatening proportions. Business strategies consistent with the Circled Wagons Strategic State may be as simple as delaying current plans or investments, or as severe as divesting a segment of the business to placate attackers or to provide revenue to stave off a takeover threat.

Short-term crises can be handled by edict management, which may involve arbitrary budget cuts or restraints placed on investment planning. Other survival techniques include financially restructuring the company, eliminating management positions or replacing leaders in the management chain, and freezing capital investment. High-level executives, including the chairman, may be called on to save the company by making public appearances or sales calls to preserve large accounts.

The collapse of Long-Term Capital Management, American Airlines during the pilots' strike, and Citigroup and General Motors during the Great Recession of 2007–2009 are all good examples of situations that required Circled Wagons strategies.

Companies seldom enter into this state deliberately. Rather, they find themselves propelled into it by circumstances beyond their control or by the accumulation of mismanaged affairs over a prolonged period of time. Perhaps the pursuit of excellence and quality was sacrificed to repair short-term profitability, or the organization was weakened by staying too long in the Slim-Down State.

Sometimes a business just fails to see the impact of events as they unfold and is caught unprepared for a major market change. In these situations, the internal or environmental problems leading a company to the Circled Wagons State usually develop unnoticed until the crisis appears suddenly—and in devastating terms.

For Effective Execution the Circled Wagons State Requires:

- Exceptional leadership to weather the crisis and lead the unit or company through bad times
- In-depth knowledge or quick access to knowledge about the core elements of the business
- The ability to salvage the right assets and position for a fast recovery

As you can see, the strategic state your business is in determines what successful execution looks like and how you get there. Effective execution in each strategic state requires that you focus on different factors. For Eagles, that focus is innovation and growth. For Forts, it's efficiency and product reliability. The Slim-Down State calls for a focus on restructuring facilities, markets and products. Finally, Circled Wagons requires a deep knowledge of the business and focusing on a fast recovery.

Despite these differences, it's important to remember that execution in each strategic state does have one thing in common: a dependence on the Five Bridges. The Five Bridges are necessary components of success in any strategic state; it's just that they're applied in a different context or environment.

Vision and Standards of Excellence

I'm not going to take time to discuss how to create a vision. Like strategic planning, that's beyond the scope of this book, and presumably, either your company's vision is already in place or you're not the person responsible for that work anyway. I do, however, need to introduce the topic so I can show how vision and plans are interrelated and how you can ensure they are aligned. The truth is, it's hard to discuss execution without mentioning vision.

How Vision Relates to Execution

A company's vision is the second outcome of the strategic planning process that has implications for execution and how success will be measured. It provides the link between strategy and action and is a prerequisite for ensuring that strategic direction and project plans will be aligned. The vision is not a pie-in-the-sky wish list, nor is it a description of an organization that is perfect in every way. Instead, it is a challenging but realistic picture of the business as it will be when the strategies have been fully implemented. It describes what the organization needs to be and is capable of becoming by a specific year in the future.

Before creating its vision, the management team should have conducted a detailed assessment of the current strategic state and expected conditions and agreed on an overall strategic direction for the business. When the management team communicates the direction and strategies to your organization, they are essentially saying, "We believe these are the right things to do—the things that will help us be successful in the future." At this point in the process, and not before, the team should begin to craft a vision of the future.

Placing the creation of the vision at this point in the process is a departure from the conventional wisdom that advocates envisioning where you want to be, and then finding ways to get there. Yes, that sequence seems logical, but it neglects to recognize that the future of any entity depends to a great extent on its past and present. What an organization is *capable* of achieving in a specific period of time is often different from what it would *like* to achieve in an ideal world—sometimes *very* different.

Here's a truism that businesses sometimes forget: to achieve you must believe. Achieving the vision depends on people's belief that it is possible. When a management team creates a vision before examining the present strategic state of the business, it risks evoking the depressing yet often realistic response: "You can't get there from here."

Want to communicate an achievable and unifying goal to your employees? Then create a vision with direct linkage to strategies—one that's inspiring because it is both challenging and realistic. The vision helps drive execution because it communicates the results an organization expects over a specific time frame and it becomes the context for organizational goal setting (strategic projects and programs, annual plan and budgets, and functional action plans). A vision looks at a selected point in the future and answers the questions: *What will we do for a living? Where will we stand in relation to our competitors? How will our customers, suppliers, and employees see us? What will we stand for?*

Here's an example of a vision developed by a large Northeast property and casualty insurance company:

> We operate for the exclusive benefit of our policyholders consistent with strong underwriting standards for P&C lines. We pursue growth in our existing products and markets without sacrificing our risk management standards. Our success depends on our people and we make every effort to ensure they are highly engaged and are learning and growing on the job. We are a dedicated member of the community and seek to improve the lives of our neighbours.

Standards of Excellence: How You Manifest Your Vision

Getting "there" (the future state described in the vision) from "here" (the current strategic state of the business) inevitably involves changing how work is done in the organization. Of course, there are a wide variety of paths to reach any goal, and choosing among them and establishing priorities is the essence of execution. It's not an easy task. Still, the process can be simplified by breaking the vision down into manageable pieces—the Standards of Excellence.

These are much more specific than the vision, and involve tangible outcomes the organization can and must achieve to ensure that the vision becomes reality. Standards of excellence describe measurable results in the areas that are most critical to the organization. For instance:

- Customers—number, mix, industry, type
- Products—number, mix, development of new products
- Performance—quality, efficiency, financial excellence
- People—hiring, development, core values
- Service—service quality, responsiveness, customer satisfaction
- Suppliers—partnerships, selection criteria, quality
- Requirements—legal, environmental, safety, financial

Essentially, these are specific performance standards that will help the organization reach its vision. In different strategic states, the standards of excellence may describe very different conditions. Excellence when you're growing looks quite different from excellence when you're shrinking or restructuring. Standards of excellence can be used to provide common goals for the entire organization, monitor progress and measure achievement, identify areas that require improvement, and set performance objectives.

In summary, standards of excellence:

- Can be observed, described, and measured
- Specify the conditions essential for the attainment of the vision and the achievement of strategic goals

- Make the vision unique and specific to your organization
- Specify what activities and outcomes will be recognized and rewarded by the organization
- Are written as performance objectives shared by the organization or for specific functions or departments
- Are used to track and monitor progress
- Are a tool for measuring current verses ideal performance

Table 2.1 shows standards of excellence and how they would be measured and monitored for the vision of the aforementioned property and casualty insurance company.

Aligning Projects and Programs with Strategy

The first step in determining what strategic projects and programs will be needed to achieve the vision and execute the strategy is a gap analysis. This is an assessment of where you are now versus where you want to be. It is the start of the transition from broader performance targets to more specific programs and projects. Once you outline the standards of excellence that will be used to measure progress toward your vision, the next step is to rate your current performance on each standard using the following scale:

1 = We NEVER meet this standard
2 = We RARELY meet this standard
3 = We SOMETIMES meet this standard
4 = We USUALLY meet this standard
5 = We ALWAYS meet this standard

Then, using the same scale, identify where you would like to be in one year on each standard. Sure, ideally, you'd like to

Table 2.1 Standards of Excellence and Measures

Standard	What to Measure	How to Measure It
Promote our products and services to existing and potential customers	• Number of products per existing customer compared to benchmark and target • Increase in revenue per product compared to benchmark and target	• Quarterly report on average number of products per existing customer • Monthly report on revenue per product
Preserve customer relationships and seek appropriate new relationships with customers	• Customer retention rate compared to benchmark • Number of new customers compared to target	• Quarterly report on customers lost and gained including the reason why
Identify and make investments that add to policyholder value	• Return on investment compared to target • Return on assets compared to target • Return on capital compared to target	• Monthly report on ROI, ROA, ROC
Create a more efficient work process through business enhancement and effective collaboration across levels, businesses, and departments	• Reliability of work process compared to benchmark • Time to respond to a customer inquiry compared to target and benchmark • Quality of collaboration across departments compared to target and benchmark	• Quarterly report on number of "errors" in work process • Quarterly report on customer response time • Quarterly pulse survey on cross organizational execution and accountability • Annual Execution and Accountability Survey

(continued overleaf)

Table 2.1 (*Continued*)

Standard	*What to Measure*	*How to Measure It*
Attract, retain, develop, and manage employees who can adapt to the changing environment and are able to support the achievement of company goals and priorities	• Employee performance evaluations • Voluntary and involuntary turnover compared to benchmark	• Distribution of end-of-year evaluations • Annual 360 feedback questionnaire • Quarterly turnover report • Talent management and succession planning process
Improve leader capability to effectively manage individuals and build high-performing teams consistent with company's leadership competencies	• Leader skill level and competence in each leadership competency • Quality of cross-organizational and intact teamwork • Employee satisfaction compared to benchmark	• Annual 360 feedback questionnaire • Elements of teamwork survey • Annual employee engagement survey
Create and sustain a culture of learning, accountability, and regulatory compliance	• Employee perception of our culture of accountability and learning • Leader behavior related to culture of accountability and employee development • Frequency and areas of non-compliance and cause	• Annual employee engagement survey • Annual 360 feedback questionnaire on relevant manager behavior • Monthly report on compliance issues

rate each one a "5." But it's best to realistically assess how much progress can be made and set priorities for those areas that will give you the most "bang for your buck" toward achieving your vision. The differences between the current and desired performance ratings will show you where the biggest "gaps" are and help you identify the standards that most urgently need attention.

At this point, you are ready to identify the specific projects and programs that will help you close the gap and reach each standard of excellence. These projects and programs will become the focus of your execution efforts. Once you know what they are, you have the information and context you need to make a strong and explicit link between specific plans and business strategy.

The Project Frame: Getting a Handle on Strategic Projects and Programs

Many of these broader strategic projects and programs will be comprised of several individual components that will require their own action plans. Yet each of these complex high-level initiatives must also be managed. All of the details can feel overwhelming. A "project frame" can help tremendously in managing and controlling the work involved in a complex strategic project as well as reviewing and evaluating the progress. An example of a project frame is shown in Exhibit 2.1.

Using a project frame to outline a high-level implementation plan for a strategic project produces benefits and supports execution at three levels. At the individual level, it provides a clear picture of the work and how it will be executed. At the group level, it encourages communication, increases the commitment to group goals, and clarifies individual responsibilities. At the organizational level, it becomes the basis for coordination and resolution of conflicts between groups.

Exhibit 2.1 Sample Project Frame

Project Name

Summarize the project's objectives with a crisp and clear project name.

Questions to Answer

- How can we immediately communicate what we are going to accomplish?

Objectives and Scope

Describe specifically what we are going to accomplish by when.

Questions to Answer

- Have the desired and anticipated results been articulated in concrete terms?
- How will things operate when the problems are solved?
- What problems, issues, units, functions, etc., are we consciously including and excluding from our projects? (What is our scope?)

Benefits and Costs

Identify and analyze the short-term and long-term benefits and costs associated with achieving the project's objectives.

Questions to Answer

- What will success look like?
- What are we trying to solve?
- What is broken?
- What needs to improve, and by how much?
- How are results tied to business goals?
- What outcomes will be important and evident to customers?
- Have we identified resource requirements (equipment, people, money, or other resources) needed to complete the project?

Key Action Steps and Responsibilities

Provide a clear picture of the work to be done and how it will be executed, and clarify individual responsibilities.

Questions to Answer

- Have we delineated the most important pieces of work to be done?
- Have we identified specific individuals accountable for results?

Monitoring Progress

Describe how progress will be monitored to ensure that the project is tracked and widely shared.

Questions to Answer

- Have milestones been set along the way, with specific progress measures and due dates?
- What measures and data will we use to demonstrate that progress is being made toward solving the problems?
- How will we know we have improved?

Potential Problems and Risk Management

Analyze the risks associated with successfully achieving the project's objectives.

Questions to Answer

- What are the potential problems?
- What is the probability that these problems will occur?
- What would the impact be if they did occur?
- What are the likely causes of these problems?
- What actions can you take to prevent them from occurring?
- What actions can you take to minimize the damage if they do occur?

Action Planning: An Execution Essential

While a project frame helps you manage and monitor the overall strategic program or project, you still need something to help manage the day-to-day execution of the project's component parts. You may have noticed that the project frame has a place to describe the key action steps and responsibilities, but these are at a very high level. Each step is so broad and complex that it needs to be broken down into smaller steps, and more detail is needed for the day-to-day management of each component of the broader project.

That is the role of an action plan. Like the project frame, it provides benefits and supports execution at three levels. At the individual level, action plans increase personal preparation by helping people think through each aspect of the project and integrate the project with other activities. At the group level, action plans capture mutual agreement on purpose, clarify individual and team responsibilities, and encourage lateral communication. At the organizational level, action plans assign and coordinate group responsibilities, become the basis for recognizing and resolving group conflicts, and help allocate resources and identify shortfalls.

Action planning is a three-step process:

1. Clarify implementation goal and standards.
2. Develop action plan.
3. Minimize risk.

Step 1: Clarify Implementation Goal and Standards. This step provides direction for the work, serves as the basis for determining individual action steps, and helps determine when a project is complete. A well-structured and useful goal statement is specific, measurable, and time-bound. It's also challenging yet realistic and attainable, consistent with available resources, and consistent with the organization's plans, policies, operating procedures and standards. To revisit our insurance company, here's an example of a well-written implementation goal it created: *Double the rate of organic growth to two thousand policies a month in the personal auto line of business.*

Similar to the standards of excellence described above, your action plan will have standards, too. They are statements of quality, quantity, and timing required for success. They drive action steps and answer the question: *What actions must be taken to meet these standards?* Outlining the standards creates an "excellence model," which describes how work will be done and evaluated. Standards for the project designed to double the rate of organic growth in the personal auto line might include:

1. Maintain current retention ratio of 97 percent.
2. Maintain safe driver criteria and keep underwriting standards uncompromised.
3. Achieve an ROI of 6 percent or greater.
4. Maintain high levels of policy holder service.
5. Provide cross-selling opportunities with other products.
6. Gain the participation and support of people and departments outside of personal lines.
7. Enhance our brand and brand awareness.

Step 2: Develop Action Plan. An action plan helps you manage the workload, review and appraise project progress, and communicate about the work to be done. Exhibit 2.2 shows the basic components of an action plan, which typically include:

- Action steps that break down the work to be done into tasks and activities
- Accountabilities that identify the individual(s) and group(s) who are responsible for doing each action step
- A schedule that includes the start and completion dates for the whole project and specific actions
- Resource requirements such as equipment, people, money, or other resources needed to complete action steps

Exhibit 2.2 Sample Action Plan

Action Steps	Resource Requirements	Accountability	Start Date	Finish Date
1.				
2.				
3.				
4.				
5.				
6.				
7.				
8.				
9.				
10.				

Step 3: Minimize Risk. Regardless of how well you have done the first two steps it takes the third one to increase the likelihood of success. Surprisingly, many people do not spend much time on this step, because they erroneously believe the development of an action plan is sufficient. Yet, no plan can truly be well-thought-out that fails to include an assessment of the potential problems that could derail it, safeguards to stave off these "what ifs," and the determination of what will be done if problems occur despite your best efforts. Exhibit 2.3 shows a portion of the potential problem analysis and steps a software implementation team took to minimize the risk to the success of their plan.

Exhibit 2.3 Sample Portion of Problem Analysis Showing Minimizing Risk

Potential Problems	Probability (High-Medium-Low)	Impact (High-Medium-Low)	Likely Causes	Actions		Accountability
				Preventive	Contingent	
1. System upgrades take longer to complete	M	H	-New version of software requires rework; -Lack of product knowledge	-Develop robust test plan; -Internal training; -Leverage vendor resources	-Replace ad hoc importing with alternative solution	Mark
2. Lack of support for scanning equipment	H	H	-Lack of internal expertise and knowledge	-Hire or outsource this service	-Line up vendor support	Carol
3. Stability issues with remote users	M	M	-Lack of clarity of user needs; -Poor performance	-Assess needs of remote users; -Ensure IT able to support needed functions	-Identify remote staff who will take on additional work caused by stability problems	Harold

47

Minimizing risk starts with a review of any circumstances that might disrupt the action plan. You can look at the plan as a whole or take each step one at a time and ask, *What could happen? What could go wrong here? What would be the likely impact?* Common "problem areas" include time, control, power/politics, resources, resistance, and stakeholders. Next, determine the probability of the potential problem occurring (high, medium, or low) and the impact if it did occur (also high, medium, or low).

Then, based on this assessment, select the potential problems that should be addressed, starting, of course, with those that are high probability and high impact and working your way down to lower levels of probability and impact. As you move down the list, due to resource and time limitations, you may decide not to work on the low-probability or low-impact problems at all.

Next identify the likely causes of the potential problems. This will help you determine how a specific cause can be controlled by preventive actions. Even if you can't eliminate a likely problem, you may be able to minimize its impact. You may decide to modify the original plan by adding or changing action steps, reassessing accountability, or changing completion dates.

Contingent actions are taken when, despite your best effort, problems actually occur. Planning contingent actions ahead of time increases the likelihood of taking effective action rather than just reacting. Contingent plans should include estimates of resource requirements and revised time frames and how to inform involved parties if the action plan changes.

The Bottom Line

Effective execution starts with a plan. And, as our research has shown, most senior teams understand that strategic planning is fundamental to success. The problem seems to be what happens, or does not happen, after the strategy is developed and people begin implementation.

The ability to effectively execute is undermined early in the implementation process for several reasons: (1) few people are in the habit of using action plans to help manage and monitor the many initiatives required to achieve a vision; (2) senior leaders fail to hold people accountable for developing and using action plans; and (3) when an action plan *is* developed, it is not always aligned with the projects that are critical for delivering business results.

These issues can be addressed, but they require a change in expectations and behavior at all levels of the organization. Make no mistake: action plans are the cornerstone of effective execution. Rather than being seen as a burden and a time-waster, action plans need to be lauded for what they can do: clarify expectations and accountability; align individuals and teams around a common objective; coordinate the effort of individuals and groups; ensure adequate resources are allocated to a project; and help you identify and take action on problems before they derail the initiative.

Such a versatile tool deserves more respect and wider use. As you progress through this book you will see exactly why. Action plans provide the context and platform for the effective use of the rest of the Bridge Builders. They help you determine when and how to apply each one. Action plans on their own won't execute for you—but, in conjunction with the other Bridge Builders, they increase the likelihood you'll execute well and obtain the results you're looking for.

Chapter Three

Bridge Builder 2: Expect Top Performance

To effectively execute plans and initiative, all team members must bring their "A" games and deliver a high level of performance. In today's lean organizations, which must accomplish challenging business objectives with fewer people, everyone needs to pull his or her weight. In other words, teams can't afford to work around poor performers.

Despite this reality, in my work with teams over the last twenty-five years I've been surprised by how tolerant many managers are of people who exhibit below-standard performance. It is almost as if they have come to accept the fact that work has to be done without the full contribution of the entire team. That acceptance is the heart of the problem.

The Pygmalion Effect: Proof That Expectations Drive Performance

It's been said that we get the direct reports and performance we deserve. I would amend this to say that we get the direct reports and performance we *expect*. But can it really be that simple? Is just expecting people to do well really all it takes to ensure that they'll deliver high levels of performance? The short answer is yes. While the idea does invite skepticism, more than four decades of research shows that when a person in authority expects others to perform well, the people under him or her actually do rise to the occasion. Let's look at three examples, among many, of the power expectations have to move performance.

Robert Rosenthal and Lenore Jacobson did one of the earliest studies of the impact of expectations on performance. It's described in their classic book *Pygmalion in the Classroom: Teacher Expectations and Pupils' Intellectual Development.*[1] A group of elementary school teachers were told that some of their students had taken an intelligence test and were identified as "late bloomers," and that these students could be expected to blossom in the coming year. In truth, the children labeled late bloomers were selected randomly and had the same average scores as the rest of the students.

At the end of the year the intelligence test was readministered. This time, the scores of the students labeled "late bloomers" were significantly higher than those of the control group. Rosenthal and Jacobson's findings have proven to be anything but an anomaly. This type of study has been repeated numerous times with the same result.

What could explain the change in the students' performance? Interestingly, when the teachers were asked, they could not recall treating any of the children differently. But clearly something was happening between the teacher and the student to cause the improvement. It seems that high expectations have a positive effect on a child's performance... but does it have the same effect with adults? A fair amount of evidence suggests that it does.

One of the more interesting studies with adults was conducted by Dov Eden and Abraham Shani and is described in their article "Pygmalion Goes to Boot Camp: Expectancy, Leadership and Trainee Performance."[2] Their study involved 105 soldiers of the Israeli Defense Forces (IDF) who were chosen to participate in a combat command course. A standard battery of tests was used to measure general aptitude, and trainees were randomly assigned to one of three groups. The intensive course involved about sixteen hours of contact daily between the instructor and the trainees over a period of fifteen weeks.

Instructors were told that considerable data had been collected on the trainees, including psychological test scores, sociometric data from the previous course, and ratings from previous commanders and that—based on this information—an assessment of the trainees' command potential has been made. Trainees were given a rating of "high," "regular," or "unknown." The instructors were told that the command potential groups were divided equally among the classes.

Next, instructors were given a list of their trainees and told to learn their names and command potential ratings. They were also told that experience with other classes had shown this assessment had predicted command potential in 95 percent of the cases. As you might have guessed, there were no actual differences in command potential among the 105 trainees.

Similar to what happened with the elementary school children, the trainees from whom instructors were led to expect more actually *did* learn more and did better on the written and performance tests. This study, however, provided additional information on the impact of the leader's expectations: Trainees of whom more was expected had more favorable attitudes about the course and more positive perceptions of the instructor's leadership behavior. Several studies conducted with other members of the IDF produced similar results.

So we see that in both educational and military settings, high expectations seem to result in higher performance. But what about civilian adults in a business environment? Does the pattern hold with them as well? A study conducted in an industrial setting by Albert S. King[3]—one of the earliest studies done with a civilian workforce—suggests that the answer is yes.

King told instructors of a welding program for disadvantaged persons that four pressers, five welders, and five mechanics were "high aptitude personnel" and that the instructors could expect outstanding performance from them. As with all the other studies, the real aptitude of the "high aptitude" designees was actually the same as that of the rest of the people in the program. And again the "expectation effect" held true: the trainees who were designated as having high aptitudes scored higher on objective achievement tests, got higher supervisor and peer ratings, demonstrated shorter learning times, and had lower dropout rates.

By this time enough work had been done on the impact of high expectations that the findings most likely surprised no one. Now, King wanted to take the research further to understand how the leader transmits his or her expectations to the direct report. To do this he used the automatic response of pupil dilations.

It's a physiological fact that when we see someone we hold in positive regard our pupils dilate without our being aware of it. In post-study interviews, King showed the trainees two pictures of their supervisors. The pictures were identical except that in one picture the instructor's pupils were normal and in the other they were noticeably larger. The welding trainees were asked two questions: whether they saw any difference in the photos, and which one "shows how you usually see the supervisor looking at you."

No one noticed any difference in the photos. Yet, remarkably, all five of the "high aptitude" welding trainees selected the photo with the enlarged pupils and five of the seven control welders selected the other picture. King concluded that eye contact—subtle as it may be—was a primary way leaders communicated their attitude, interest, and expectations for the direct report. Later studies have shown that other forms of interpersonal communication like listening and feedback are also ways leaders communicate expectations.

The phenomenon we see played out in these studies is called the Pygmalion Effect or self-fulfilling prophesy (SFP). The name is based on the myth of Pygmalion, who carved a statue of a woman so beautiful that he treated it as if it were alive. The goddess Aphrodite took pity on Pygmalion and magically brought the statue to life. A more contemporary reference is the George Bernard Shaw play of the same name on which the movie *My Fair Lady* was based.

Here's an interesting finding that came out of the body of SFP research: while people in the "high expectation" groups rated the instructor more positively than people in the control groups did, the leader did not recall treating people differently. This implies that having high expectations has a subconscious effect on leader behavior. It causes leaders to unknowingly treat the people from whom they expect higher performance differently than they treat the rest of the group. Conversely, when the leader expects little, he or she does little to facilitate success. Feeling neglected and discouraged, these people are more likely to flounder and fail.

Again, all of this takes place without the leader realizing it is happening.

So what does all of this mean for 21st century business leaders? It means, quite simply, that expectations matter. Although we might want to believe that high expectations alone are sufficient to improve performance, it is difficult to make a rational case for that. However, it is also difficult to deny that there is some meaningful connection between the expectation of the leader and the performance of the employee.

> High expectations for performance appear to affect both the leader and the employee. It causes managers to treat employees differently and provide support and feedback. It builds self-esteem in the people from whom more is expected. And it creates an environment conducive to performance, one in which employees demonstrate increased confidence and try harder.

"But I Know Them Too Well"

So the key to enhancing your team's performance is simply a matter of raising your expectations for people and treating them as if you believe they are capable of meeting those expectations...right? Well, yes, as far as it goes. Unfortunately, raising your expectations is easier said then done.

Even when we meet someone for the first time, we tend to form an impression about that person's capability based on some stereotype (neat people are well organized) or bias (senior citizens are resistant to change). It's not fair, but it's hard to avoid. So when we're dealing with a person whose habits we know all too well—when stereotypes and biases don't even factor into our judgment—it's even more difficult to change our expectations.

Think about it. When you've worked with someone for months or years, you may have too much evidence of his performance (either barely at or below standard) to see him as anything but a marginal performer. Dov Eden, author of *Pygmalion in Management: Productivity as a Self-Fulfilling Prophesy*, calls this a self-sustaining prophesy.[4] Because you have an impression of the person performing at a certain level, you continue to expect less from him and in return you get less.

Breaking the low expectations/low performance cycle is very difficult. In fact, in all the studies on the self-fulfilling prophesy, the leader's expectations had to be manipulated. They were told something that was not true about a person's capability or potential. As effective as this appears to have been, it would, of course, be unethical outside an experimental environment. So what can you do when you want to set higher expectations for someone for whose upper limit you feel you already know?

Breaking the Cycle

There are three techniques you can use to help see marginal performers in a more positive light and deal with them in a way that sincerely communicates your confidence in their ability to meet higher expectations. Just to be clear, they can be used with poor performers *and* with those who are meeting current expectations but whom you feel could come to exceed them. These techniques are described below.

Technique 1: Assume Value

Think about your interactions with your below-standard performers and see if this is true. Once you believe that someone is not competent, it seems that everything he says or does is wrong or stupid. He just cannot produce a worthwhile suggestion or idea because everything he says or does is seen through the lens of our low expectations. The starting point of breaking the cycle of low expectations is to assume value and listen for the positives.

This requires more than self-discipline, although that will come into play when you hear an idea that reinforces your low expectations. How can you respond to an idea that seems to be totally unacceptable in a way that maintains the other person's self-esteem and still gets the idea over our "threshold of acceptability"? It's called a "balanced response" and it is the best communication tool you will ever use. When used effectively it's almost like magic.

A balanced response is a technique for responding to an idea that appears unacceptable without being confrontational or diminishing self-esteem. The balanced response identifies the "pluses" and the concerns about performance or ideas in a way that encourages problem solving. It allows strengths to be leveraged regardless of weaknesses, allows weaknesses to be overcome without losing sight of strengths, highlights points of agreement, and positions concerns for problem solving.

A balanced response has two parts. First, state what you like about the idea—the positives. Sample lead-ins for presenting positives include, "What I like about your idea is...," "The benefits are...," "The strengths are...," and "What I found especially helpful is...." Doing this forces you to focus on the positives and helps you avoid a knee-jerk reaction to critique or reject an idea that sounds ridiculous to you.

Please understand: the intent is *not* to lull the person into complacency so you can more easily get the negative comments under his guard. In fact, the positive comments need to be substantive and related to the issue at hand. For example, it would not be effective to say, "I'm glad that you've been coming in on time" when the idea is about changing the format of a monthly report. The message you want to communicate is that, although the idea may not be totally acceptable in its current form, there are some aspects of the suggestion you find useful and they are a good place to start a conversation.

Second, state what you see as the key concerns—what, in your opinion, keeps the person's idea or performance from being totally acceptable. State these concerns in an actionable, "How to" form and avoid using the word "but" to transition from your positive statement to your constructive one. Sample lead-ins might include, "How can we . . . ?" "What I'm concerned about is . . . " "Some things that might be improved on are . . . " and "I wish we could . . . ."

There should be only one or two critical concerns on your list, and they should be related to the positive comments you just made. For example, "I like the idea of changing the monthly report to a quarterly report because it would allow us to allocate the time to more important activities. I am concerned about the impact the change could have on our customers who have come to expect to receive the information on a monthly basis." This allows you to get your concern on the table and turns the conversation to how to make it work rather than rejecting the idea completely.

Technique 2: Focus on What They Do Well

Even your worst performers do something well. If you can't think of *anything* a person does well, you have a different problem. Find the thing your marginal employee currently does well, no matter how small, and focus on that. Start where you and she have confidence in her ability to deliver results and move out from there. Set a modest stretch goal that is easily attainable and provide the appropriate coaching and support as she takes the risk and tries something new.

Because you are building from a base on which the person has succeeded, she may see it as a modest risk and be more willing to put in the effort required for success—and you may be able to be more authentic when you provide support and express your confidence that she can succeed.

Technique 3: Make the Unconscious Conscious

Based on the self-fulfilling prophesy research, the key to helping people meet your higher expectations is to take whatever you, the leader, appear to be doing subconsciously and make it a more deliberate process.

Here is the real question: What are leaders who have positive expectations actually doing to create such a dramatic impact on employee performance? The work of Rosenthal and Rubin[5] and Eden[6] indicates that when leaders have high expectations they tend to more frequently demonstrate five leadership competencies: enhancing the other person's feelings of importance and self-worth, encouraging people to step out of their comfort zones, creating a supportive environment that is safe for risk taking, reinforcing positive behaviors and clarifying what "good looks like," and providing feedback that is balanced and constructive.

Let's take a closer look at each one.

Enhance and Maintain Employee Self-Esteem. We are motivated to work at a level consistent with our perceptions of our own competence. Our level of performance is more often determined by our subjective beliefs in our ability to perform, rather than by objective conditions. In short, when we feel competent, we are much more likely to perform competently; when we feel incompetent, we are less likely to succeed.

Strengthening a person's belief in his own competence is a foundation of effective management, and managers have significant impact on their direct reports' perceptions of competence. When we erode our direct reports' self-esteem, their productivity and performance are likely to decrease. When we enhance their self-esteem, their motivation to perform competently increases. Makes sense, right?

Few managers *intentionally* say or do things to lower the confidence and erode the self-esteem of their direct reports. It is not typical (although certainly not unheard of) for a manager to say something like, "You're stupid and just don't get it."

What's more likely is that we believe our comments or actions are benign or even helpful, when in fact, they are confidence killers. These comments are usually much more subtle though no less devastating. For example, statements that tend to erode self-esteem include:

- "I gave the project to John since he always does a great job."
- "This project may be too complex for you."
- "On the last three projects, you haven't sought any opportunity to expand your role. I just want you to know that I'm aware of that."
- "I want you to realize that this is the second time we've discussed your customer-relations skills. I don't intend to discuss them again."

On the surface these comments sound rather harmless. They may even reflect the manager's attempt to be clear about expectations and performance—to be a "straight shooter." But let's compare them to examples of comments that tend to maintain self-esteem:

- "What are your ideas on improving your level of market knowledge?"
- "You're 10 percent over budget for this project. How can we bring costs under control?"
- "Last time we spoke, you said you felt an 8 percent increase in productivity was reasonable. However, the department is at 2 percent. What has happened since we last reviewed this issue?"

Notice the difference? These statements still point out deficiencies and problems. The manager is not avoiding a direct conversation but has found a way to raise the concern in a less punishing way. Her tone is focused on problem solving and her approach is more participative. By focusing on the problem and not the person, the manager is able to address the issue without eroding her direct report's self-esteem. In addition, by asking the person how he would handle the situation and involving him in determining the solution, the manager both signals that she has confidence in the person's ability and uses the interaction as a coachable moment.

Set Challenging Goals. Giving people a chance to work on tough assignments and setting challenging goals are concrete expressions of your confidence in them. Performance improves because specific objectives guide effort toward productive activities and challenging objectives tend to energize a higher level of effort.

The purpose of a challenging goal is to encourage people to step out of their comfort zones, energize them, and build confidence. You want to find the right balance of difficulty and feasibility so you challenge and stretch the person without demotivating or discouraging her.

> To determine whether a goal is challenging but realistic, look at both the person's ability and the difficulty of the task. A goal is probably too easy if there is little or no improvement in expected performance when conditions become more favorable, or if it calls for a level of performance below that of most other people in a comparable situation. On the other hand, it's probably too difficult if it calls for a level of performance well above her prior levels when working conditions are stable or worsening or if the expected level of performance is well above that of other people in a comparable situation.

For most of us, it's pretty much a no-brainer to set challenging goals for easily measured aspects of the work, such as quantitative outputs like sales or the number of widgets produced. We have a harder time setting clear and challenging expectations for areas that are more difficult to measure—like service quality or customer satisfaction. As a result, we either avoid these areas or allow them to remain in the "I'll know it when I see it" category. Either approach limits your perspective, inhibits your ability to set high expectations for key elements of the work, and makes it tough to hold people accountable.

It helps to remember that although some objectives are "measurable" the attainment of all objectives is "verifiable." For example, customer satisfaction levels can be determined by surveying or interviewing customers about their perception of key elements related to satisfaction—ease of use, freshness, speed, product performance, and so forth. The extent to which service quality goals are being met can be verified by comparing *actual* service to an agreed-on set of service standards like responsiveness, the effective handling of problems, on-time performance, and availability of products.

Perhaps you are familiar with the concept of SMART goals. Even if you are, a brief overview is appropriate because these guidelines are an excellent way to ensure that the goals you establish are clear and high quality and that they motivate people to step up to the challenge. SMART goals also ensure there are no misunderstandings about what is expected so that follow-up conversations will be constructive rather than frustrating or punishing.

Smart goals are

- **Specific.** Goals should be expressed in terms of a specific outcome or result for which the person will be held accountable and should answer the following questions: *Is it precise enough to establish clear expectations? Does it identify what actions will be taken? Does it specify the outcomes that will result (such as what we will see as a result of the expanded effort)?*

- **Measurable.** Goals should be expressed in terms of an outcome that can be measured or otherwise verified. Measures include quantity and quality standards, turnaround time, and budget guidelines.

- **Aligned.** Goals should be consistent with the organization's strategic objectives. During the goal-setting process, help the person understand your business objectives. This helps ensure that the goals she creates in collaboration with you are directly linked to business objectives and, ultimately, the organization's strategic objectives. Putting the goal in this broader context motivates her to put in the necessary effort because it gives the goal meaning and relevance and helps her understand how what she is doing contributes to business results.

- **Realistic.** Goals should be challenging but realistic given the current environment, available resources, and the person's experience and skill level. The following questions will help gauge whether the goal is too challenging or unrealistic: *Are the resources available to realize the goal? Will the person have the necessary authority to make required decisions and actions? What assumptions have been made (for example, about uncontrollable variables)? Do these goals create too much stress? Are the goals appropriate for her experience and skill level?*

- **Time-bound.** Goals should include a target date or deadline by which they will be met. It is also useful to specify shorter, trackable segments that will enable you to check progress. The following questions will help determine whether appropriate and realistic timeframes have been established: *Should review discussions or status updates be scheduled separately from other ongoing performance discussions? What are the logical checkpoints and major milestones where progress will be reviewed? Can progress be divided into logical stages for assessment? What information will be needed for a complete* *picture of progress, and how will it be obtained? What alarms will alert us if we are off-track?*

Create a Supportive Environment. A supportive environment encourages people and makes them more comfortable with trying new behaviors and taking on challenging assignments. The existence of this type of environment is directly related to the leader's behavior. Supportive leadership involves a variety of behaviors by which you show consideration, acceptance, respect, and concern for others. Making eye contact is one example. Other supportive behaviors include restating someone's comment in your own words to check for understanding, giving encouragement when a person has a difficult task, offering to provide advice or assistance when someone needs help with a difficult task or problem, and being patient and helpful when giving complicated explanations or instructions.

Supportive leadership conveys positive regard for others and shows that you view them as worthy of respect and consideration. The use of supporting behaviors builds and maintains effective interpersonal relationships. It's also strongly related to satisfaction with the leader. Obviously, it's more satisfying to work for or with someone who is friendly, cooperative, and supportive than with someone who is cold and impersonal, or worse, hostile, uncooperative, and does not treat others with respect.

Effective leaders spend time with direct reports and colleagues to get to know them better and relate to them as individuals. In the process, there are opportunities to build mutual respect and trust that will provide the basis for a cooperative working relationship. The emotional ties you create will make it easier to gain the cooperation of people on whom you rely to get the work done.

Ask yourself: *How do I react when a colleague or direct report is upset or worried about some aspect of the work?* By listening attentively and trying to show that you understand what a person is saying and feeling, you communicate concern and the desire to be helpful. Effective leaders are able to suspend their biases and preconceptions, make an active effort to understand and appreciate why someone is upset, and provide appropriate support.

Catch People Doing Something Right. Although it's a simple act, providing recognition for a job well done has a powerful effect on people's performance. It reinforces good work and shapes future behavior. It motivates, builds trust, and builds self-esteem and confidence. It makes people more receptive to feedback for improving performance.

When done well, recognition is more than just a "psychic hug" that makes a person feel good about himself (although that is also a desirable outcome). When you give recognition you are sending two important messages to anyone who is trying to meet the higher expectations and challenging goals you have set. First, you're helping him understand what "good" looks like. When you recognize someone's behavior or output, you clarify and reinforce what the expected standard of performance should be. The message is, "This is what it looks like when it's done well, so keep on doing it."

To determine what contributions and accomplishments merit recognition, you must have a model in your own mind of the behaviors that are important for success and consistent with the values of the organization: teamwork, customer service, open communication, respect for people and initiative, for example. In order to obtain improved performance you need to be specific about what you would like to see improved. If you cannot name the behavior, he cannot change or improve it—or in the case of recognition, continue to use it.

The second message is, "You can do this." Recognizing calls the person's attention to the fact that she has accomplished something important or made meaningful progress. Recognizing builds self-esteem and confidence, improves job satisfaction, and encourages her to expend extra effort toward performance targets.

Recognition should be given when a direct report:

- √ Does something you would like him to repeat
- √ Accomplishes something that was difficult for him
- √ Meets or exceeds his goals
- √ Completes a development goal
- √ Demonstrates a competency effectively
- √ Shows initiative in coming up with innovative ideas or in solving problems
- √ Goes the extra mile
- √ Takes appropriate action to support team plans and goals
- √ Takes a prudent risk
- √ Makes progress in learning and demonstrating new skills or knowledge
- √ Achieves a milestone in pursuing a long-term or complex plan or goal
- √ Improves his performance

Recognition should be given even if the person has not achieved the performance standard but has made significant improvements in performance. Why? Because this encourages and strengthens efforts toward additional improvements. Recognition of improvement is especially relevant for new employees or employees who do not have much self-confidence.

Surprisingly, despite its potential to shape behavior and build self-esteem, recognizing is one of the most underutilized leadership behaviors. Many of us tend to notice and criticize ineffective behavior, but fail to notice and praise effective behavior. We mistakenly believe bringing performance problems to a person's attention will prevent them from happening again. While critical feedback *can* be an important part of performance management, it's more effective to reinforce positive behaviors that should be repeated.

In the words of Ken Blanchard, it's important to "catch people doing something right." Ralph Gonzalez, a store manager with Best Buy in Florida, took this idea very literally and with great results. Ralph was charged with turning the store around. To drive home the point that it is possible to find examples of excellence anywhere, he celebrated every small achievement. He also gave all employees whistles and told them to blow the whistles every time they caught someone doing something that supported the turnaround.

In short order the store became one of Best Buy's best stores as measured by almost any metric: sales growth, profit growth, customer satisfaction, or employee retention. As Ralph Gonzalez demonstrated, recognition does not take much time and costs little or nothing, yet has a powerful impact on execution.[7]

Generally, businesses use three types of recognition: awards, recognition ceremonies, and praise. Awards and recognition ceremonies are often formal programs. In contrast, praise is usually an informal activity and provided directly by the manager.

Praise is more likely to be successful if it is specific, relevant, and timely. It is not enough to simply say, "Good job," "Keep it up," or "Nice work." Instead of a general comment commending someone for carrying out an assignment or completing an initiative well, it is better to explain what the person did well and why it is important to the team or organization. There are several reasons why.

First of all, describing the person's behavior and the beneficial impact it had will clarify why the behavior was deserving of recognition. Specific praise is more believable than general praise because it shows that you actually know what he's done and you have a sound basis for a positive evaluation. Otherwise, the employee might think you are just "blowing smoke" or "tossing him a bone." In addition, citing specific examples of effective behaviors communicates what behaviors you value and guides him toward repeating those behaviors in the future. For example:

- Make a general statement about the performance being recognized. "You made a very effective presentation to the customer on Friday."
- Describe specifically what he said or did that contributed to the positive results. "You were well prepared and very convincing about what's in it for them. In addition, you anticipated, responded to, and overcame their objections when you said . . . ."
- Describe the specific positive impact of his or her performance. State how the person's performance positively impacted his or the team's performance, achievement of goals, and the business. "Based on your effective presentation, we were able to gain the customer's commitment to accept your proposal which will result in . . . ."

Finally, research shows that praise is more effective when provided soon after desirable behavior occurs, rather than waiting until a future time, such as saving it for the annual performance appraisal.

Employee recognition is more art than science. There is no simple, mechanical formula for determining what type of recognition to use. It depends on the type and importance of the accomplishment to be recognized, the norms and culture of the organization, and the characteristics of both leader and recipient.

> Whatever form of recognition you use, it must be sincere. Most people are able to detect efforts to manipulate them with praise or rewards. Avoid overusing a particular form of recognition or recognizing someone too frequently for the same thing. Do anything too often and its effect can become diminished.

Provide Constructive Feedback. Recognition is only half of the feedback equation. In addition to what they are doing well, it's important to provide people with balanced feedback—in other words, to give them information about what they need to do better or differently. Feedback is most effective when it is

- Focused on behavior within the person's control
- Focused on one or two important issues, rather than several trivial ones
- Descriptive rather than evaluative
- Specific
- Prompt rather than delayed
- Done in a way that encourages two-way communication
- Collaborative with regard to the solution
- Focused on the future and not on the past
- Balanced—meaning it includes strengths and weaknesses so that people understand what to keep doing and what to change

Two techniques will help ensure your feedback is constructive and increase the likelihood that it will be accepted and used: (1) focus on behavior and (2) use the Situation-Behavior-Impact Model. Here's a little about both:

Focus on Behavior. When discussing performance expectations, be specific about what the person is doing or saying. This puts the focus on her behavior or actions, rather than on her attitude or personality, which is likely to provoke defensiveness. If your boss told you that you "lack commitment," you would not know exactly what you needed to do differently. To improve your performance you would need to know what you said or did that indicated to your boss that you lacked commitment. Are you arriving late to meetings? Are you missing deadlines? Are you failing to provide team members with needed information or updates?

Furthermore, such a label runs the risk of triggering an emotional reaction (anger or resentment) that could negatively affect the person's performance. Therefore, to communicate clearly and effectively, focus on the specific behavior—what the person is or is not doing or saying.

Here's a simple test that can determine whether you are at the behavior level or whether you are using more general characteristics or labels. Before you give the feedback, ask yourself, "What did the person do or say that indicated that she _____ [fill in the blank with the characteristic or label you are thinking of using, for example: "has a bad attitude," "procrastinates," "is uncooperative," or "is not doing the full job"]. Keep asking the question until your answer is the basic unit of behavior and it does not make sense to ask the question again. For example, if your answer to the question "What did she do to make me think she was procrastinating?" is "She did not hand the report in on time," you know you're at the behavior level because asking the question again will not yield anything more specific.

Use the Situation-Behavior-Impact Model.[8] Just like praise (positive feedback), effective constructive feedback also has three components: the situation (Under what circumstances did you observe the person's behavior?), the behavior (What, specifically was he or she doing? What are the observable actions and verbal and nonverbal behaviors that need to be changed or improved?), and the impact (What were the consequences of this behavior on you, on others, on the person's results, the department's goals, or the project?).

Here is an example:

> "I'd like to debrief today's sales presentation, Tom, and the way you dealt with the client's cost objections. You were very clear about the benefits and you were able to demonstrate the value we bring relative to the competition. I do have a concern about the quality of the pitch book. There were several typos in the

introduction and you had to explain the incorrect projections in the chart on page 9. Those kinds of mistakes impact the customer's confidence in our ability to deliver what we promise. If we can't get the presentation right, how can they expect us to get their order right?"

Being balanced—describing both effective and less effective behaviors—accomplishes three objectives: you reinforce behaviors she should continue to use, you clarify what needs to be done differently, and you minimize potential defensiveness. By focusing on impact you describe how the specific behavior affects others or the organization; for instance, poor documentation can affect others who rely on that documentation for accuracy. This helps the person see the importance of addressing that behavior and ensures that the feedback is non-evaluative.

It also helps the person see that you did not bring up the subject just because of your personal preference for how something should be done. Describing the impact takes the behavior out of the realm of opinion—which can be debated and for which there may be several points of view—and puts the behavior in context of an objective result.

The Bottom Line

In today's competitive business environment you need every member of your team working at full potential. Incredible as it may seem, having high expectations and sincerely believing that people are capable of meeting your expectations actually results in improved performance. The evidence is overwhelming. When we believe people are capable, we treat them like they are capable and they come to believe they are capable. Unfortunately, the converse is true as well. This powerful dynamic starts when your expectations (high or low) are translated into behavior.

The real challenge of using high expectations to improve performance and enhance execution comes not when we meet someone for the first time but when we have a preconceived bias based on stereotypes or observation of past poor performance. If we are to execute effectively, we *must* stop perpetuating self-sustaining prophesies. We *must* stop ignoring people we believe are not capable or reinforce their self-concepts through our comments (or lack thereof).

By assuming value, focusing on what they do well, setting realistic but challenging goals, providing recognition and feedback, and creating a supportive environment where it is safe to try new things, we can enhance the self-esteem of our lower-performing or average employees. We can increase their willingness to put in the effort required. Ultimately, as they show improvement, we can come to sincerely believe that they are capable of doing the full job or exceeding standard levels of performance. And when all of these conditions come together, we can create a team of higher performers—a team that can execute more effectively than ever before.

Chapter Four

Bridge Builder 3: Hold People Accountable

In the social sciences we spend our time trying to understand and predict human behavior. We often find ourselves in envy of the physical sciences. They, after, all can point to phenomena in nature that are predictable and constant, such as what happens to water when it's exposed to a specific temperature or pressure. Unfortunately for us, human beings do not lend themselves to that kind of predictability and consistency. It's tough to make a definitive statement about what a person will say or do in a specific situation.

I believe, however, there is at least one principle of social science that is predictable and consistent. On employee surveys, when you ask people whether they and others in their department are held accountable for results, you always get a very high percentage of favorable responses. However, ask them whether people in other departments are being held accountable and the percentage of favorable responses is typically very low.

In other words, while we believe *we* take accountability for our actions, we are just as certain that *others* do not. This is one aspect of human behavior that you can take to the bank.

Watching the behavior of our elected officials, business leaders, and athletes, it's hard not to wonder why some people refuse to be held accountable for their actions and their impact, while others are willing to step up and take full responsibility with no excuses. (*Yes*, there are some honorable individuals in all of these professions.)

To answer this question let's start by clarifying what we mean by accountability and what it looks like in practice. Here is one example. On the same day Robert Rubin moved from the job of chairman of the executive committee to chairman of the board, Citigroup announced that it had $55 billion of collateralized debt obligations (CDOs) and other subprime-related securities on its balance sheet and that an estimated $8 billion to $11 billion of write-offs were imminent.

Rubin was a risk wizard at both Goldman Sachs and the Treasury, and some questioned why he didn't do something to help avoid both this disaster and earlier write-downs that Citigroup reported. Although Rubin had restricted himself to a non-operating role at Citigroup, mainly advising the CEO and dealing with important clients, a reporter from *The New York Times* asked him how this CDO exposure could have gone on under his nose.

"The answer is very simple," he said. "It didn't go on under my nose." Rubin went on to explain that you have people who are specifically responsible for certain areas and you have senior management making sure that they are qualified for the job and monitoring their work. "I am not senior management," Rubin said. "I have this side role. I tried to help people as they thought their way through this. Myself, at that point, I had no familiarity at all with CDOs."

Rubin seems to be ready to provide several reasons why he cannot be held responsible for Citigroup's CDO problem, despite his background, experience, and his central role at the bank.[1]

On the other hand, American sprinter Tyson Gay is a good example of someone who does not blame poor performance on outside factors. America had high expectations for Gay's performance at the 2008 Summer Olympics, but his 10.05 in the 100-meter dash ended his chance at winning an individual gold medal. Gay had strained his left hamstring at the U.S. Olympic trials. He did not run a race between that time and the Olympics and he spent the month with a noted sports orthopedist.

After the race, Gay said, "I may have needed more races, but I don't really have any excuses. I just didn't make it. My hamstring feels good. It's not bothering me. I don't have any type of excuses. I wasn't too overwhelmed with it being the Olympics. It's just one of those things that's happened."[2]

If that was not enough of a disappointment for Gay, six days later during the 4 x 100 relay he and Darvis Patton botched the handoff of the baton that kept the U.S. from qualifying for the 400-meter relay final. They both took responsibility. "I take full blame for it," Gay said of his bad exchange with Patton. "I kind of feel I let them down." Gay said he felt the baton but "then I went to grab it and there was nothing. It's kind of the way it's been happening to me this Olympics."[3]

Now, let's contrast Gay's attitude to what we see around us every day at work. How big a problem *is* the lack of accountability in today's organizations, anyway? Our research suggests it's a fairly substantial one.

> In our survey of over four hundred senior and mid-level leaders, 40 percent report that employees in their organizations are not being held accountable for results and 20 percent report that managers in their organizations do not deal with poor performers. It also appears that the presence or absence of accountability in an organization makes a difference — 77 percent of leaders in top-performing organizations report that "employees at all levels are held accountable for results," compared to only 44 percent in less-successful organizations.

What *Is* Accountability Anyway?

Many people think of accountability only when something goes wrong or when someone else is trying to pinpoint blame. Actually, accountability has far broader implications.

Phillip E. Tetlock, a Mitchell Professor of Organizational Behavior, Hass School of Business at the University of California at Berkeley, has done extensive research on why we do and do not take accountability and the impact accountability has on our performance. He notes that taking accountability is related to the expectation that others will observe our performance, that what we say or do will be linked to us personally, that our performance will be assessed according to some normative ground rules with implied rewards and consequences, and that we expect to have to give reasons for what we do or say.[4]

Accountability is good for us and for our companies. Tetlock's study of seventy-two undergraduates at the University of Southern California shows how accountability enhances individual performance by motivating us to engage in more complex and vigilant information processing, inspiring us to exercise more caution in making decisions based on incomplete information, and making us more receptive to information that challenges initial beliefs.

In the study, students received a booklet containing a description of the most important evidence of a court case where a Mr. Smith had been charged with the murder of a Mr. Dixon. Half the arguments in the booklet implied the defendant was guilty and half the arguments cast doubt on the defendant's guilt.

Students were randomly assigned to one of three groups. The "no accountability" group was assured prior to reading the evidence that their impressions of the guilt or innocence of the accused would be totally confidential and not traceable to them personally. Before reading the case materials, the "pre-exposure accountability" group was told that they would be asked to justify their impressions of the accused person's guilt or innocence. People in the "post-exposure accountability" group received the same information, but only after they had read the case material.

Finally, the information was presented in one of three orders: evidence suggesting guilt before evidence suggesting innocence, evidence suggesting innocence before evidence suggesting guilt, and a random alternating order of both types of evidence.[5]

In an interesting commentary on how we process information and make decisions, Tetlock found that information presented earlier had significantly more influence on the perception of the person's guilt than the information presented later (more people perceived Mr. Smith to be guilty when they received the evidence suggesting guilt first). However—and this is even more interesting—the phenomenon occurred only when people did not expect to have to justify their opinions or if they found out they would have to justify their impressions *after* they read the evidence.

Telling people prior to reading the evidence that they would have to justify their impressions appears to make them more cautious about jumping to conclusions from incomplete data and makes them more willing to consider contradictory evidence when it's presented later. In addition, people who knew they would have to justify their views *prior* to seeing the evidence recalled significantly more case information than those who knew they were unaccountable or who found out they would be held accountable *after* reading the evidence.

Increased accountability also seems to enhance team performance. Team members who are held accountable rely on each other more, experience more success, and express more satisfaction with the members of their teams than those who are not held accountable. Patricia Fandt—a professor of management at the University of Central Florida whose research focuses on accountability and team development—conducted a study that supports this assertion.

She gathered data from 460 managers who participated in a ten-day training program that was designed for groups of twenty to twenty-five people in which participants worked in teams of four or five on complex task assignments. In the high-accountability teams, participants were told that both team and individual performance evaluations would be reviewed by their immediate supervisor. In the low-accountability teams, participants were told that they were not accountable to their supervisor for individual or team performance evaluations.

The high-accountability teams were more likely to have team members who worked interdependently, which led to higher success and greater satisfaction. The bottom line? By increasing team and individual accountability and encouraging people to take responsibility for their decisions, organizations can have a highly positive impact on team performance and improve its ability to execute plans and initiatives.[6]

Why We *Should* Hold People Accountable —and Why We *Don't*

When we fail to hold others accountable, we reap the consequences—some obvious, some not so obvious. A lack of productivity is one of the more obvious negatives that come to mind. While everyone is busy pointing fingers at others, deadlines don't get met, the work remains below standard, or customers continue to be dissatisfied. Worse yet, things won't get better until people stop trying to affix blame and start addressing the issue that caused the problem in the first place. This cycle will continue until people take accountability for their contributions to the problem and focus on seeking solutions.

The impact that a lack of accountability has on your top performers is a little less obvious. What happens when someone (often a chronic poor performer) drops the ball and we don't hold her accountable for results? We usually give the assignment to someone we feel we *can* count on and ask him to make it right. This may work in the short term, but in the long term it creates more problems than it appears to fix.

First, asking your top performers to pick up the pieces will eventually wear them out. They may very well come to see their heavier workload as punishment for good performance. In addition, taking a poorly executed assignment away from someone just reinforces the poor performance. The message is, "Don't worry if you screw up. You won't be asked to make it right because someone else will get the assignment." For unmotivated employees, the lighter workload that results is, in effect, a reward for poor performance.

In my view, the greatest impact of not holding others accountable is that it creates a negative perception of the leader. When other members of the team see you letting someone get away with not producing the agreed-on output or keeping commitments, they begin to wonder why they are working so hard. They wonder why you don't take action to address a poor performer who is creating problems for the rest of the team.

Yes, failing to hold others accountable reflects on you as a leader. It raises questions about your willingness to hold everyone to the same standards and creates the perception that you don't treat people fairly and equitably. Pretty soon others on the team get the message about "what it takes to succeed around here" and the extent to which they can count on you as a leader.

Lack of accountability creates and reinforces a culture of blame—which, in turn, generates other problems. You may notice increased evasion and avoidance as well as a pervasive "don't get caught" attitude. Innovation plunges as people become less willing to be creative and think out of the box. Employees take fewer risks (or stop taking them altogether) because no one wants to be blamed if something goes wrong. "Blamestorming" sessions proliferate, creating a cycle of blame that ultimately shuts down communication.

So here's the real question: if accountability is critical to execution and individual and team performance, then why *don't* we consistently hold people accountable for results? There are several reasons. In fact, I believe there are seven assumptions and misunderstanding—let's call them "Tickets to Slide"—that contribute to this phenomenon.

Ticket to Slide 1: "This Too Shall Pass"

The "wait and hope" syndrome assumes that poor performance will improve on its own over time. "They'll learn," we say, in the (often futile) hope that we'll never actually need to have a conversation about meeting commitments and delivering results. Or you assume that people know what they should be doing, and that this was simply a blip on the radar screen. "I'll give him the benefit of the doubt this time," you say. Problem is, "this time" often turns into "next time" followed by "What? It happened AGAIN?"

Ticket to Slide 2: "They Know How I Feel"

You just responded in your "I'm dissatisfied" voice and put on your "I'm very disappointed" face. That should do it, right? Well, maybe not. Most of us like to assume that sending indirect messages and subtle signals has not only made our dissatisfaction known but clarified what needs to happen differently—and how it needs to happen. Yes, it's a highly unlikely outcome, but many of us prefer it to a more direct discussion of the problem and the need to take responsibility. Unfortunately, it seldom works.

Ticket to Slide 3: "It Will Turn into an Argument"

Even if the other person is not difficult to work with, it's a safe bet that he or she will likely have a different point of view. You are certain this will deteriorate into an uncomfortable conversation or, worse yet, a real disagreement. Better to let it go and avoid the conflict. But while it may be easier in the short term to "just let it go," in the long run you may find that the situation has snowballed into a problem that is vastly more difficult to deal with.

Ticket to Slide 4: "I Made My Expectations Clear (I Think . . .)"

One reason you may avoid holding others accountable is that, actually, you have *not* set clear expectations. Either you haven't clarified what you want done, what "good looks like," or when you want it done. Without this base, don't be surprised when you encounter more than one point of view or when conversations turn into arguments. Remember: *everything* can be either measured or known. Even qualitative outputs such as customer service or quality have components that we use to know when they have been done well. Those are the things for which we can set expectations and monitor and measure.

Ticket to Slide 5: "I Will Demotivate or Lose Them"

One of the challenges managers face is holding top performers accountable for behavior that is consistent with work processes and organizational values. You may be inclined to give these "superstars" some leeway because you feel they're too important to your team's success and you don't want to break their momentum or steal their mojo. Unfortunately, this sets up an undesirable dynamic among the team where people come to believe that it doesn't matter *how* you hit the target—as long as you do, you're not accountable for other aspects of performance.

Ticket to Slide 6: "I Will Be Seen as a Micro-Manager"

Over the years consultants and academics have put the fear of micro-managing into the hearts of many leaders. We avoid the implication of it at all costs. In a world where a "collaborative" style is revered and a "command and control" style is frowned upon, the practice of monitoring has an undeserved bad name and has fallen out of favor. The truth is, the more you delegate and empower others, the more you need to monitor and track progress. Following up and monitoring progress are not synonymous with micro-managing. Monitoring, when done well, can be a constructive activity that provides an opportunity to make course corrections and praise good performance.

Ticket to Slide 7: "It's Easier If I Just Do It Myself"

Doing it yourself may seem like a good idea when you're making the call, but few myths are as wrong as this one. When you don't hold others accountable and you take on the work yourself, you become complicit in the cycle of poor performance and lack of accountability. If you do not break this negative cycle, you will *always* have to do it yourself because you've missed a coachable moment and an opportunity to set expectations.

Assessing Accountability: The Four Levels

Joan Didion said, "Character—the willingness to accept responsibility for one's own life—is the source from which self-respect springs." I agree. And the willingness to accept responsibility does more than build self-respect, it sets us up for greater success. Conversely, the less willing a person is to take responsibility, the less successful he or she will be—in the workplace and in society in general.

Bruce Fern and Herb Cohen of Performance Connections have developed a four-point scale that can be used to measure your own level of accountability or to assess the level of accountability of the people with whom you work.[7]

Level Four: Accepts Responsibility for Actions and Impact

The primary focus of the highest level of accountability is on both actions and the consequences of those actions. When things go wrong, people operating at this level acknowledge how their behavior contributed to the cause of the problem and accept the consequences of their behavior with no excuses. Typical language might be, "I took those actions and I am responsible for the outcomes of my actions."

Tiger Woods demonstrated level four accountability at the 2009 British Open. Woods is generally considered the world's leading golfer, yet that year he failed to make the cut by one stroke. "Obviously it's very disappointing," Woods said of his performance. "I was playing well coming in, and today, unfortunately, I just did not play certain holes well."

Although Woods could have used bad weather conditions as an excuse—"The wind was blowing pretty good," Woods said. "It was coming off the left pretty hard."—he didn't blame them for his poor performance. Instead, he chose to take full accountability for the quality of his game and the consequences. "You just had to hit good shots and I did not do that," Woods continued. "It was a crosswind with holes that go from left to right, and it was coming over your shoulder. You've got to hit some good draws in there and hold it against that wind, and I didn't do that."[8]

Level Three: Accepts Responsibility for Actions But Not Impact

At this level we are still in positive territory. The primary focus of Level Three individuals is the acceptance of accountability tempered by a desire to explain the influencing factors. In other words, they accept responsibility but want others to understand why they made the choices they did. Although people at this level are explaining the causes of their inability to meet expectations, their intent is more about solving problems than making excuses. Typical language at this level might be, "Yes, I did those things. Here are some of the factors that influenced the situation."

Former Federal Chairman Alan Greenspan, who retired in 2006, was a long-time supporter of deregulation and it was that philosophy that guided his eighteen-year stewardship of U.S. monetary policy. Once heralded as the driver of the world's longest post-war economic boom, he was taken to task by the House oversight committee looking for answers to an economic crisis triggered by a disturbing level of financial risk taking.

Although Greenspan did state that he regretted his opposition to regulatory curbs on certain financial derivatives, he wanted people to understand what went wrong and why he was not fully responsible for the consequences of his actions. "Those of us," he said, "who look to the self-interest of lending institutions to protect shareholders' equity are in a state of shocked disbelief."

When asked directly if he was wrong, Greenspan replied, "I made a mistake in presuming that self-interest of organizations, specifically banks, is such that they were best capable of protecting shareholders and equity in the firms ... I discovered a flaw in the model that I perceived is the critical functioning structure that defines how the world works. I had been doing this for forty years with considerable evidence that it was working exceptionally well."[9]

Level Two: Acknowledges Involvement But Deflects Responsibility

At this level we are moving into negative territory, accountability-wise. For people operating at Level Two, the primary focus is on deflecting responsibility. They may acknowledge their involvement but express frustration with others who dropped the ball and rationalize their own responsibility and involvement. Typical language at this level is, "I did do it, but, but, but ... " or "I was involved, but I'm not responsible."

In 2007, the extent to which the infrastructure in the United States had deteriorated became apparent when the news hit that the Interstate I-35 bridge in Minnesota had collapsed. When asked about her role in the tragedy, Carol Molnau, the lieutenant governor and transportation commissioner, revealed herself as a master of responsibility deflection.

Despite being head of the Minnesota Department of Transportation, Molnau claimed she was not making decisions and shifted blame to others. Specifically, she said the decision not to reinforce the I-35 bridge was made by engineers working with an outside firm. "Of course I'm not the one making the decision," she said. Molnau also blamed a lack of transportation resources on federal earmarking.[10]

Level One: Acknowledges Absolutely No Accountability.

Here, the primary focus is on denial and blaming others. People at this level may demonstrate extreme defensiveness, saying things like, "I had nothing to do with it—it was him, not me."

The fall of Lehman Bros., a venerated 158-year old Wall Street institution, shocked almost everyone and, some believe, may have been the event that set the credit crisis in motion. Over-exposed in the high risk subprime mortgage market, Lehman lost $3.9 billion after taking a $5.3 billion hit on the value of its portfolio of residential mortgages and was forced to file for bankruptcy when the U.S. government would not provide the funds to bail them out.

Testifying before Congress, Richard Fuld, Lehman's CEO, said, "I wake up every single night wondering what I could have done differently." He also said he felt his decisions were "prudent and appropriate." He went on to explain why the demise of Lehman was not his fault and blamed almost everyone and everything else for Lehman's problems, including the Federal Reserve, short-sellers, a systematic lack of confidence, the media, and inconsistent regulation.[11]

Obviously, not everyone is going to operate at the higher levels of accountability all the time. But most people can learn to move to higher levels at least *some* of the time. It's one thing to determine what level of accountability a person operates on, but here's what most leaders want to know: *Can I help the people on my team become more accountable and stay that way? And what can I do to achieve this goal—especially in regard to the people who regularly deny or deflect responsibility?*

The good news is you can help people increase their levels of accountability. Later in this chapter we'll review two proven techniques for doing just that—we'll call them *Accountability Boosters*. One technique sets people up for success, minimizing the likelihood that there will be a problem or failure in the first place. The second encourages and enables people to take accountability for their actions and the consequences when, despite your and their best efforts, something goes wrong. These techniques also help you move a person from Level One or Two to a Level Three or Four.

As a start, it helps to understand why people make excuses in the first place. If you are familiar with the four "Excuse Factors" we're getting ready to describe, you can take steps to remove them or to minimize their impact.

Why We Make Excuses

Listening to the news or observing colleagues and direct reports at work can, at times, be both frustrating and depressing. When asked to justify a decision or explain why something did not happen as planned, many people feel compelled to explain why it was not their fault—and if only they had known a particular fact or if only someone else had done something differently, the less-than-ideal outcome could have been altered.

We've all heard the excuses. Excuse making, it seems, is a way of life for many people. In fact, acknowledgement of accountability has become such a rare event that when someone actually does the right thing, we feel compelled to heap praise on that person. Why is it so tough for people to kick the excuse habit?

Research on excuse making points to four factors that explain why, when things go wrong, many of us seek to deny involvement, blame others, or explain why things were beyond our control. An understanding of these factors—preserving self-image, the degree of identifiability, unforeseen consequences, and locus of control—provides the foundation for effectively managing accountability in ourselves and in others.

Excuse Factor 1: Preserving Self-Image

It's a well-documented phenomenon: most people think of themselves as superior to others in areas that are important to them such as intelligence, creativity, or a particular technical skill. When we feel responsible for a negative outcome, it strikes at our core sense of self. We are generally motivated to present ourselves favorably to others and, when this self-image is threatened, we compensate by taking credit for success and disavowing failures.

Research has found that we also tend to shift the reasons for negative outcomes to sources that are less threatening to our self-image. For example, instead of saying, "I did not complete the project on time because I have poor project management skills," we might say, "I did not complete the project on time because I could not get the information I needed." Although this still acknowledges participation in creating the problem, it minimizes our direct responsibility and focuses on a cause that is less threatening to our self-image.[12]

Excuse Factor 2: Degree of Identifiability

People tend to exert less effort and take less accountability for individual and team performance when doing work as part of a group rather than acting alone. This tendency toward what has been called "social loafing" is well documented. In these cases, some of us may take advantage of a situation in which it's harder to pinpoint responsibility—a situation created by the fact that many people have a role in the team's performance.

This low degree of "identifiability"—when our individual performance is not clearly observable—allows us to more easily "hide" and avoid taking accountability for our role in the team's poor performance. However, when identifiability is high—when others *can* see our individual performance and our contribution is clearly linked to us—accountability and performance levels both increase.

One example of the impact of identifiability on accountability and performance comes from a study done by Kipling D. Williams of Purdue University and his associates that looked at the times of sixteen members of the Ohio State swim team in a competitive event. Four teams of four men were formed by matching for ability and speed of each swimmer's time for a 100-meter lap.

Two of the four teams were randomly assigned to the "high identifiable" group, whose lap times would be announced aloud to them and to anyone else within hearing. The other two teams were assigned to the "low identifiable" group, whose lap times would not be announced or revealed, even if the swimmer asked for the information. Each swimmer raced two 100-meter individual freestyle events and two 400-meter relay events (where each team member swam 100 meters).

Williams found that identifiability did have an effect on the level of effort exerted and, as a result, the swimmer's times in both the relay and the individual events. As you might expect, when swimmers' scores *were not* made public, they exerted less effort and swam both the individual and relay events more slowly. When individual scores *were* made public, the swimmers exerted more effort and swam faster in both events.

The surprising twist here is that when individual scores were made public for the relay and the individual events, individual swimmers were faster in the relay (a team event) than in the individual event. Williams speculates that the faster times in the relay when identifiability was high could be the result of swimmers feeling more pressure from their teammates than when swimming individually.[13]

It appears that the stakes are higher when we know our action will be attributable to us and that we have to justify ourselves and our actions to others. Knowing this, we seek approval and respect and try to maintain our own self-image—we try harder. In these cases, however, excuse making is also more likely if we do not perform to our own and others' expectations and if we believe that failure will lead to some form of criticism or punishment.

Excuse Factor 3: Unforeseeable Consequences

Excuse makers often attempt to shift responsibility from internal to external causes. One way they do this is to deny intentionality for poor performance by insisting, "But I didn't *mean* to." The assumption (a widely held one, by the way) is that unintended actions are not as bad as intended actions and do not deserve as severe a punishment. In addition, because people are held more accountable when the consequences of their actions were clearly foreseeable, they feel their best option is to justify and explain their behavior when things go wrong.

People who are held accountable for unforeseeable consequences will be especially likely, and quite legitimately, to make excuses. Tetlock found that excuses and denials of responsibility peak when decision-makers expect to explain to an evaluative audience why they made less than optimal decisions and when they didn't have sufficiently useful information on which to base them. In this situation, excuses and explanations may be justified and help minimize the tendency of members of the evaluative audience to claim the certainty of their current perspective or awareness in hindsight—the belief that "What I now know, because it seems so obvious, I actually knew all along."[14]

Excuse Factor 4: Locus of Control

What does "locus of control" mean? Basically, it refers to the extent to which you believe that your destiny and behavior are guided by your personal decisions and efforts or the belief that it is guided by fate, luck, or other external circumstances. This belief, and the actions that are consistent with it, is referred to as your "locus of control." We all fall somewhere along this continuum.

When you believe you have the power to control your own destiny and determine your own direction, you have an *internal* locus of control. A recent story in *The New York Times* about Skip Watkins' struggle to find a job during the Great Recession of 2007–2009 and his eventual success, illustrates what an internal locus of control looks like. He was laid off from his job as a vice president of technology in the gas chromatographs division of Xiotech in August of 2008 and did not find work until February of 2009. In his interview he said, "I feel fortunate to have found another job, but I've never considered myself a lucky person. I got to this point through hard work."[15]

Those of us with an internal locus of control tend to see the world through a more adaptive perspective. We believe that hard work and personal abilities will lead to positive outcomes. People with an internal locus of control tend to engage in activities that will improve their situation and try to figure out why things turned out the way they did. Because such people believe they control their destiny, they are less inclined to make excuses and more inclined to take accountability for their actions and the consequences that follow.

An example of a strong external locus of control—in this case, a very extreme example—is Jason Rodriguez. Rodriguez was arrested for shooting six people, one fatally, at an Orlando, Florida, office building where he once worked. For two years he had been having a difficult time finding work, after being fired from an entry-level job at an engineering company where the shooting took place. According to the arrest records, Rodriguez told the police, "I'm just going through a tough time right now, I'm sorry." When asked by a reporter why he opened fire, he replied, "They know why I did it; they left me to rot."[16]

Rodriguez appears to believe that he does not have control over his destiny and that it is guided by external factors. Clearly, he feels that his current problems have been caused by someone else—some outside group or individual—and does not recognize how his actions might have brought him to this point in his life.

Perhaps you've seen these four factors play out inside your own company. Maybe one of your top performer's self-image is threatened when his idea does not produce the intended results and he becomes defensive. Or you've heard someone complain that because she can't control all the elements of a project she should not be held responsible if things don't go right. Or it suddenly becomes clear that the ability to disappear into the group is allowing someone to avoid taking accountability for his lack of individual contribution.

As I mentioned earlier, the following Accountability Boosters will help you accomplish two important objectives—(1) minimize the need for people to make excuses in the first place and (2) increase their level of accountability when things go wrong.

Accountability Boosters: Managing Accountability in Others

Many of the negative assumptions we make about holding others accountable and the reasons why we make excuses can be addressed and managed via a two-part process. The first and most important part is setting people up for success by avoiding four accountability mistakes leaders commonly make. The second part kicks in when something goes wrong despite everyone's best efforts. At that point, the objective is to help and encourage people to take responsibility without making them feel worse than they already do and to focus on problem solving and making the event a learning experience.

Before-the-Fact Accountability Booster: Set People Up for Success

The best way to manage accountability is to ensure that people follow through in the first place, versus trying to hold them accountable after they've dropped the ball. That means avoiding certain "accountability busters" on the front end.[17]

- Accountability Buster 1: Talking about an idea, but not agreeing to actions and accountability by people's names, and people thus assuming someone else is going to do something.

- Accountability Buster 2: Agreeing on an action, but without any discussion of a completion date, so the end date is open to interpretation and differing opinions.

- Accountability Buster 3: Waiting until the completion date to check on the results, or not even checking in at all.

- Accountability Buster 4: Not holding people accountable for missed commitments after the fact.

Three techniques can help you avoid these mistakes and dramatically increase the chances that people will follow through and keep their commitments. Fern refers to them collectively as the ATC Model and compares managing accountability to the work of an air traffic controller: "Just as air traffic controllers have to juggle different flights simultaneously to make sure every flight lands safely, you must help your direct reports, peers, and even your manager juggle their priorities to ensure every commitment they make 'lands safely,'" he says.

The three techniques are clarifying actions and expectations, agreeing on due dates for deliverables, and establishing check points. The acronym ATC (air traffic control) can help you remember the technique.[18]

Action. This is the starting point both for setting people up for success and for being able to hold them accountable after the fact, so it is critical to get it right. This is where you clarify expectations (what "good looks like") and identify who is accountable for which parts of the work. Regardless of how good an idea someone has or how sincere her intention, nothing happens until someone commits to taking some action to produce a specific deliverable.

It is unfair to expect someone to deliver the results you expect if those results are not outlined clearly and unambiguously. In fact, if expectations and responsibility for specific aspects of the work are up for interpretation, it's impossible to hold someone accountable for results. Missing this first step often explains why many managers are hesitant to discuss accountability when people do not follow through or, when they do, why the conversation can deteriorate into "he said, she said" arguments.

Timetable. Just as important as clarifying actions and expectations, establishing an agreed-on due date is critical to ensuring everyone is on the same page. Due dates like "as soon as possible" and "by next week" lay the foundation for misunderstandings because your "as soon as possible" may not be anywhere near someone else's. (Does "by next week" mean *before* next week? Does it mean Monday of next week or Friday of next week?) In addition, commitments that don't have a time frame frequently do not receive attention and usually fall by the wayside.

Checkpoints. One of the biggest mistakes people make is waiting to check in until the action or deliverable is due. Although the pitfall seems obvious—waiting until the due date to check in does not leave time for problem solving—it is surprising how many people stumble into it. One explanation leaders offer for this self-defeating behavior is that they're afraid of communicating a lack of trust in the other person's ability—or of being labeled a micro-manager.

The simple, yet powerful, solution is to establish periodic progress check points before the due date. The frequency of the checkpoints will depend on the difficulty of the task and the experience of the person. This technique simultaneously solves both problems: the implied lack of trust and the micro-managing.

Agreeing on checkpoints with the other person makes follow-up and progress checks a shared and mutually endorsed activity. The check-ins are now part of project management, and they also provide opportunities for you to coach if there is a problem and recognize and reinforce behavior when things are going well.

In addition, because you've outlined the milestones you are comfortable with and built in time to get things back on track if you discover there is a problem, you don't have to give in to the temptation to make spontaneous or surprise visits or to call when you get nervous about whether the project is on track.

After-the-Fact Accountability Boosters: Two Responses to Missed Targets

Sure, prevention is better than an after-the-fact remedy. But in the real world, people *will* drop the ball from time to time. When this happens, there are two strategies you can use to increase accountability: asking three accountability questions and reducing defensiveness.

Ask Three Accountability Questions. Rather than berating a person for her failure to deliver results, reinforce her accountability and focus on problem solving. Three questions will encourage the person to think about how she contributed to the current situation, what she can do to get things back on track, and what she can do to prevent it from happening again.[19]

In addition to asking these questions directly yourself (which might come across as accusatory), you should coach the person to pose them to herself as a way to manage her own accountability. The three questions are:

- *Present:* "What can I do now to get on track?"
- *Future:* "What can I do to prevent this problem from happening again in the future?"

- *Past:* "What could I have done to prevent the problem? What, if anything, did I do that might have possibly contributed to the problem?"

The first two questions are less likely to evoke a defensive response, but the third one might very well push that button. Be prepared to deal with defensive behaviors.

Be Aware of Defensiveness and Reduce It. Defensiveness is the accountability killer. As I mentioned earlier, people become defensive and deny accountability in order to maintain their self-image as a competent person or to avoid negative consequences. Blaming people for being defensive usually makes them even more defensive. There are, however, several things you can do to avoid a defensive response or reduce the other person's defensiveness when it occurs.

The best strategy is to avoid a defensive response in the first place. The ATC model sets the stage for clear conversations and ensures there will be time to solve problems and make course corrections before the deadline. The three accountability questions enable you to get at the issues without being overly critical or resorting to assigning blame, which helps maintain the person's self-esteem and general feelings of competence. The focus on problem solving enables you to have a more constructive conversation and allows the person to participate in developing a solution that should help him put aside his concern about punishment.

If an employee does demonstrate defensiveness, don't let his attitude "push your buttons" and cause you to become angry or more strident in your efforts to convince him that he should take responsibility and own the problem. Actually, the best way to handle the situation is exactly the opposite—by demonstrating empathy. Calling the person's attention to his defensive response and demonstrating your understanding of the reasons for it help diffuse the feeling and enable both of you to focus on solutions.

> Naturally, you want to move things along and avoid having to deal with what you might consider whining and excuses. That's why, in response to defensive comments — for instance, "I couldn't have known," "I didn't do it on purpose." "This is not what I intended," or "It wasn't my fault" — you might be inclined to say, "Look, we agreed on the objective and you agreed to take the point on the project. That's the past; now we have to just focus on fixing it." Don't do it. This type of comment just fuels the defensiveness as people try to justify their actions.

As much as many of us would like to pretend that emotions are not part of work, they are. That means it's going to be harder to help the person focus on solutions until you get the "feelings" part of the discussion out and resolved. A more effective response might be, "I know you're as concerned as I am about this and I realize it's not the way you wanted things to turn out. This conversation is not about assigning blame. It's about solving the problem and ensuring that we keep it from happening again." Comments like this make people aware of their defensive response, assures them that you understand their point of view and how they feel, and clarifies that your objective is to find a solution and not to assign blame.

Once the person is aware of his defensiveness, the three accountability questions outlined above can be used more effectively to facilitate a constructive discussion. As a last resort, if he continues to make defensive comments and cannot focus on the problem at hand, you may want to use the 24-Hour Rule—suggest taking a break until the next day. This gives him a chance to think and cool down and come back to it later when he's ready.

The Bottom Line

For me, a high level of accountability often looks a lot like what we call "initiative." At work, people who have a high level of accountability will take initiative to ensure the success of a project, provide early warning of potential problems, and take action to resolve a problem, even if it is not their fault.

Although we are aware that it's important, many of us still hesitate to hold others accountable for their actions. In the heat of the moment, it may seem faster and less of a hassle to let something go or to wait and see what happens. However, those of us who are "one-trial learners"—meaning we don't have to experience something more than once to get the lesson and change our behavior accordingly—know that this approach does not work in the long term.

One reason we hesitate to tackle the accountability problem in a timely way is a lack of clarity on what the person is accountable for in the first place. Discussions about accountability can be straightforward and potential conflicts less intense when everyone knows ahead of time what is expected and how success will be measured. Plus, of course, establishing this clarity reduces the likelihood of having to have the discussions in the first place.

Taking accountability comes naturally to some people. For many of us, however, the more natural tendency is to justify and explain why we are not responsible when things go wrong. Although you cannot change human nature, those of us in a managerial or leadership role can help create an environment that enables others to operate at a higher level of responsibility. The key is setting people up for success by clarifying expectations up-front and building in time for course corrections before the deadline. This helps avoid the need to make excuses because problems are identified and solved before the due date.

When targets are missed, three accountability questions—*What can you do right now to get back on track? How did you contribute to this situation? What can you do in the future to ensure this will not happen again?*—can be used to solve the problem, rather than trying to pinpoint blame. This approach helps minimizes the threat to the person's self-image. The three questions, along with techniques to effectively deal with a defensive response, also minimize the need to make excuses as you and the other person collaborate on finding a solution.

Chapter Five

Bridge Builder 4: Involve the Right People in Making the Right Decisions

Effective execution and the delivery of consistent results depend on getting the right people talking about the right things at the right time. But that's only part of the equation. You also need to increase the likelihood that those "right people" are using good judgment and making the right decisions. Three factors contribute to achieving these outcomes: (1) having the right balance of centralized and decentralized responsibility, (2) ensuring the right people are involved in decisions, and (3) adopting processes that ensure that high-quality decisions are being made.

Although it was one of the five differentiators of companies that are most effective at execution, only 54 percent of participants in our study responded favorably to the item, "My company has the right balance of centralized and decentralized responsibility to achieve the strategy." Clearly, many organizations struggle with this issue.

As we mentioned earlier in this book, when Mark Hurd became CEO of Hewlett-Packard he decentralized the sales organization to create this balance and to align responsibility for business development and customer satisfaction with each division. But the centralized/decentralized decision-making balance isn't just about improving organizational efficiency. It's also about clarifying responsibility and ensuring the right people are involved in making key decisions. Hurd's change in structure supported his objective of increasing accountability and putting decision making in the hands of the people closest to the problem.

However, because this book is intended for people who deal with execution day-to-day—and who, while they might be able to "fiddle" with organizational structure, probably don't have Hurd's leeway to impact it to a great degree—the focus of this chapter will be on what middle and first-line managers can do to ensure that the right people are involved in decisions and that good decisions are being made.

As straightforward as this sounds, it is not that easy to achieve. In our study, only 47 percent of participants reported that they were appropriately involved in decisions. Furthermore, when you look at how the human brain works and the impact that has on our thought process and our judgment, it is amazing that good decisions ever are made.

Okay, that last statement is somewhat of an exaggeration. After all, good decisions *do* get made every day. The question is, how does that happen given the obstacles created by organizational structure and the psychological challenges we face as we process and react to information? And the bigger question is, how can we make it happen more often?

This chapter will review the factors that affect our judgment and decision making, for better and for worse, and provide guidelines based on what effective managers do to improve judgment and increase the frequency with which good decisions are made.

Job 1? Empowering others.

Beyond the Buzzword: What "Empowerment" *Really* Means

As we said, the right balance of centralized and decentralized structure helps put decisions in the hands of people closest to the problem. Still, that's only part of the solution. These people must be given substantial responsibility for meaningful tasks and the information and resources needed to implement them. Plus, they must be trusted to solve problems and make decisions without obtaining prior approval.

Examples of empowerment can be found in many companies. Often, they involve front-line employees who have direct contact with customers. When British Airways allowed its customer service representatives to deal with each case individually, rather than following rigid protocols for handling complaints, customer retention rate doubled to about 80 percent.[1]

Jetway Systems yields another example. Employee Dan Brown designed a console pre-tester on his own initiative, preventing delays that were costing the company up to forty-eight hours worth of time for remanufacturing consoles found to be defective further down the assembly line. The device resulted in a savings of $20,000 over the first six months.[2]

Many companies, however, don't seem to have as solid a grasp of the concept.

Over the last decade the term "empowerment" has become widely used, and leaders at all levels have been challenged to do more of it. And that, I believe, is part of the problem. The ambiguity of the buzzword is likely to send some leaders down the wrong path and invite outright rejection from others. (When it's tossed around with no explication, it can sound off-putting and trendy.)

From my point of view, the term does not improve communication or clarify what you need to do to "empower" others. You may have noticed in the description above that empowering includes two practices that have been on the list of managerial success factors for decades; delegating and informing. Labeling these core managerial practices "empowerment" does not appear to add any real value and only contributes to distracting and misleading observations like, "You can't empower other people, they can only empower themselves."

To me, this argument seems more like a rationalization for why it's not the manager's problem when direct reports fail to take the initiative to resolve issues and make decisions on their own.

Empowerment should be seen as an outcome, not a behavior in and of itself, which directly results from the manager's interaction with his or her direct report. Lest I sound too curmudgeonly, I do believe the word is a useful shorthand way to talk about what effective managers do to ensure the right people are talking about the right things—as long as we recognize that delegating, informing, and trust are required to achieve that outcome. That is how I use it here.

The Core of Empowerment: Delegating and Informing

In today's organizations leaders are neither able nor expected to do everything themselves. The nature of our work world makes that impossible. Substantial delegation is essential in fast-changing environments that require high initiative and a quick response by front-line employees. The same is true of organizations that have flattened their hierarchies and increased the number of people reporting to each manager.

However, people are unlikely to be successful in carrying out a delegated task unless they are given adequate resources, clear objectives, and appropriate authority and discretion. Failure may also result if people lack sufficient expertise and essential skills or if they are already overloaded with other tasks and cannot get any relief or assistance with them. Table 5.1 shows the characteristics of effective delegation compared to less effective attempts.

Delegation involves giving people the discretion to determine how to do a task without interference. What it *doesn't* mean is relinquishing all responsibility. To achieve the potential benefits of delegation, you must find a good balance between autonomy and control.

Monitoring too closely suggests doubts about the abilities of the person or team assigned to the task. It sends an "I don't trust

Table 5.1 What Effective Delegation Is—and Is Not

Dump and Run	Effective Delegation	Over-Engineered
In This Approach to Delegation the Leader . . .	In This Approach to Delegation the Leader . . .	In This Approach to Delegation the Leader . . .
• Waits until the last minute to assign tasks • Omits important details about the job • Doesn't provide needed resources • Assumes that the person will "figure things out" and answer his or her own questions • Assigns jobs to people who aren't competent to do them • Lets go too soon; doesn't check in or monitor progress • Seems oblivious to feelings about the job	• Provides enough lead time for tasks to be done right • Provides relevant facts and the big picture • Provides needed resources • Provides time to ask questions and figure things out • Assigns jobs to people who are competent to do them • Lets go, but is still available to help; monitors progress without micro-managing • Builds confidence and competence with sincere feedback	• Provides so much lead time that there's no sense of urgency • Provides every detail, leaving no room for creativity • Provides too much information • Tries to answer every question, even before it's asked • Assigns jobs to people who are overqualified and will be bored • Doesn't let go; micro-manages • Gives too much praise over trivial things

you" message. On the other hand, abdicating all responsibility may contribute to frustration and even failure. It's best to agree up front on the amount of discretion that will be allowed and ensure it reflects the skills and experience of the people who are empowered.

Of course, all the empowerment in the world won't help your cause if the people you've delegated to can't make good choices.

And that leads to a crucial question: Why do people make the choices they make—and how can we influence them to make good ones?

Brain Basics: How Cognitive Systems Impact Judgment and Decision Making

Many people from different disciplines have spent a lot of time trying to understand how we make decisions. Economic theory, for instance, would have us believe that we make choices based on a rational evaluation of the consequences. Yet years of research within psychology, supported by neuroscience, finds that the way we go about making decisions isn't always rational. Nor is it the result of a single cognitive process.

> Although there is still much to learn, we now know that decision making is a very complex process that involves interaction among multiple subsystems of the brain, each of which is guided by different parameters and principles. Alan S. Sanfey — a cognitive neuroscientist and professor of psychology at the University of Arizona and an expert on how neural processes affect decision making — and his colleagues use the analogy of a modern corporation to explain how the brain works. Both are complex systems of specialized functions that transform inputs into outputs. Both have hierarchical structures and rely on executive systems that make judgments about the relative importance of tasks and decide how to mobilize specialized capabilities to perform these tasks.[3]

And how do our minds navigate these complex systems to reach a decision? Well, a new approach known as *neuroeconomics* offers an explanation. It integrates ideas from psychology, neuroscience and economics to explain how the multiple, diverse, and specialized neural systems of the brain coordinate their activities and affect our judgment and choices. As we'll see shortly, in some instances this interaction among neural systems might be better described as competition. Let's look at two pair of neural systems that have significant impact on our judgment and the quality of the decision we make—*automatic reactions and conscious processing* and *emotion and deliberation.*

Automatic Reactions and Conscious Processing

Automatic reactions, such as recognizing a face, are learned responses based on experience that quickly propose intuitive answers to problems and situations as they arise. These are the actions and choices that kick in when a situation seems familiar. As the label suggests, automatic reactions require little or no conscious thought.

Conscious processing, such as reasoning, is our conscious and voluntary information manager. It is slower to engage and can only support a small number of tasks at a time, while multiple automatic reactions can be carried out simultaneously.

Sanfey uses the analogy of driving a car with a stick shift to illustrate the differences between automatic reactions and conscious processing. A student driver relies on conscious processing, which is concentrating on a sequence of steps that take effort to perform. These steps can be articulated and are easily disrupted by distraction. An experienced driver, on the other hand, relies on automatic reactions. Although he may not be able to describe the individual operations, he can drive the car while carrying on other activities like drinking water or talking to a passenger.[4]

The stick shift example also illustrates that activities and choices can become automatic with training or experience.

It appears, however, that conscious processing accounts for only a small part of our overall behavior and frequently struggles to compete with our automatic reactions. In general, conscious processing functions as the monitor and regulator of our automatic reactions. Think about it this way: our actions and choices are initially determined by automatic reactions, and conscious processing kicks in only when we "pause" because we perceive that the cost or impact of an automatic reaction may be too large. In these situations the advice we received from our parents would apply—think before you act.

Look at brand loyalty, for example. We go to the supermarket and buy the same brand of orange juice or cookies every time. We recognize the label and make the purchase without paying attention to the price or nutritional content. Why should we? We've bought this product for years. So we continue buying this product almost on autopilot—until we realize that the cost has increased 25 percent or until the high amount of fat and cholesterol is brought to our attention. Once we're aware of the impact of "not thinking before we act," we are much more likely to start reading labels and comparing products for price and nutritional value.

A story in *The New York Times* shows what can happen when our automatic reactions are *not* checked and balanced by our conscious processing. The number of banks taken over by the Federal Deposit Insurance Corporation (FDIC) grew rapidly in 2009 but not because they were involved in exotic financial instruments. Instead, the failures were due to the enormous volume of loans that went bad.[5]

How did bankers who were smart enough to stay away from strange securities and "stick to their knitting" find themselves with loan losses that greatly exceeded their available capital?

Here's one explanation: the absence of problems early on was taken as evidence that nothing bad was going to happen. Because bankers "learned" that they were able to take greater risks with minimal losses year after year, they responded in an automatic fashion to situations that looked familiar rather than evaluating each loan on its own merit.

In other words, although these bankers may have been aware of the potential downside of their actions, the lessons learned through experience diminished the ability of their more thought-ful conscious processes to get adequate consideration and put a check on risky behavior.

There are, however, situations when letting automatic reactions guide our behavior without the regulatory effect of conscious processing works in our favor—when acting without (or before) thinking is actually best. The stick shift analogy is one such situation. Clearly, it makes for safer driving when you can direct your attention to the road rather than concentrating on how to use the clutch and switch gears.

Another example can be found in *Sources of Power: How People Make Decisions*. In it, author Gary Klein describes his years of studying how people use their experience to make decisions in field settings (rather than the laboratory). He began studying firefighters and later moved on to pilots, nurses, military leaders, and chess masters, among others.

In his first study of firefighters, Klein asked an experienced commander to describe some difficult decisions he has made. He was surprised to hear the commander say that he did not make decisions. Upon further observation Klein realized that, in an emergency, the commander did not have to compare alternatives because he was able to come up with the best course of action from the start. He was able to do this each time the situation changed, which of course tends to happen in crises. Even in a complex and changing situation, the commander could see it as familiar and know what to do.[6]

Emotion and Deliberation

The brain also has separate systems that support *emotion* and *deliberation*. Emotion refers to psychological processes that are triggered by events and information and that result in a behavioral response. For example, a threatening situation such as seeing a bear lumber out of the woods and head for your tent would trigger the emotion of fear, which might cause you to run away as fast as you can—which might not be the best course of action.

Deliberation, like problem solving and planning, are more rational and take a long-term view of the consequences of our behavior.

As much as we would like to approach decision making in a rational, logical, Mr. Spock–like manner, we frequently find our emotions coming into the picture. And that's not necessarily a bad thing. In fact, research indicates that emotions may actually enhance our decision-making ability.

The work of Antoine Bechara—a researcher working out of the Department of Neurology at the University of Iowa who used a gambling task to understand the role emotions have in our decision-making process—seems to support this point.

The study involved people with damage to the ventromedial prefrontal cortex (VM), which means they have difficulty with decision making but not with other intellectual functions, and a control group of people with normal brain function. Participants were told that the goal of the gambling task is to maximize profit and they were given $2,000 in play money as a loan. They were asked to pick one card at a time from one of four decks and were told that each time they could pick from any deck they wanted. With each turn the person either received money or was asked to pay a penalty.

Two of the decks of cards had high gains and larger losses (A and B) and the other two (C and D) had smaller gains and smaller losses. For example, a person might have turned ten cards from deck A or B and earned $1,000 dollars, but she might have also received five penalties for a total of $1,250, incurring a net loss of $250. For decks C and D, after turning ten cards the person might have earned $500 but the total penalty would only have been $250, for a net gain of $250.

The game required a person to choose between imme-diate and delayed reward or consequences without knowing future outcomes (in this case, how many rounds she would play)—conditions that very much reflect real life. Bechara found that the people with normal brain function avoided the "bad" decks (A and B) and more frequently selected the "good" decks (C and D), while the participants with brain damage did not display this tendency.[7]

So why *weren't* the VM patients able to make better choices? To find out Bechara had the two groups perform the same gambling task while hooked up to a machine that measured their skin conductance response activity (SCR), which increases as stress and the moisture on your palms increases. Both normal participants and VM patients generated SCRs after they were told they won or lost money.

More importantly, however, the normal group began to generate SCRs *prior* to selection, as they were deciding from which deck to choose. These pre-selection SCRs were higher before selecting a card from the "bad" decks. VM patients did not generate any SCRs before picking a card.[8] Based on these results, it appears that emotional signals that are generated in anticipation of future events can guide decision making.

Unfortunately, this isn't a hard-and-fast rule. Emotional signals can also work against us. Take, for example, the decisions people make when they participate in "The Ultimatum Game," which has them negotiate with one another. In this two-player game, one person has a sum of money—say $10—to split with the other person. Player 1 can offer any amount and keep the rest, but only if the offer is accepted. Player 2, the recipient, can reject any offer but then no one gets anything.

The theory is that if the people were acting rationally, Player 2 would accept any amount offered even if it was small, because getting something is better than nothing. But in reality, it didn't always work that way. When Sanfey scanned the brains of the players, he found that as offers became increasingly unfair, parts of the brain involved with emotion and reason became more active. They seemed to be competing for influence—*Should I take an insulting offer or punish the offerer?* When the emotional areas dominated the deliberative areas of the brain, the player rejected the offer and no one got anything.[9]

Here's another example of how emotion can cause us to ignore available data and deviate from optimal behavior. Camelia Kuhnen, a professor at the Stanford University Graduate School of Business, and Brian Knutson, a professor in the Department of Psychology at Stanford, designed a task to elicit risk-taking and risk-avoiding choices. Over several rounds subjects were shown two stocks and a bond and asked to choose one. After a brief waiting period their earnings for that round and their total earnings were displayed, along with the results from other possible choices.

The game was set up so that outcomes of some "good" stocks were better than other "bad" stocks and bonds had 100 percent probability of providing a positive outcome, but at a much lower rate than stocks. Kuhnen and Knutson monitored the relevant areas of the brain and found that one area activated before risky choices (those with high potential gain and high potential loss) and risk-seeking mistakes (making poor choices when taking too much risk for a potential gain) and a different area activated before riskless choices (those with no or low potential loss and low potential gain) and risk-aversion mistakes (poor choices made when trying to minimize the risk of losses). The results demonstrated that the emotional anticipatory brain activity of either gain or loss promotes decisions that are not always based on the available data and excessive activation in either of these areas often led to mistakes.[10]

The behavior of individual investors during the financial crisis of 2007–2009 shows what can happen when emotions override deliberation and available data is ignored, causing us to make less than optimal choices. In 2007, when the stock market started on a significant decline, some people were so concerned about locking in losses that they refused to sell their stocks, even as bad news continued to emerge and they continued to lose money.

The inverse is also true. During the upturn that started around March of 2009, many investors were so traumatized by their previous loss experience and fearful that they refused to reenter the stock market even as positive news about the economy became available and they watched the S&P Stock Index climb over 50 percent in nine months of that year.

So How *Can* We Make Better Decisions?

Understanding how the brain processes and responds to information and how this impacts our judgment and decision making can help us improve our own decision-making processes and those of our employees. Making complex choices whose outcome is uncertain requires both broad-based knowledge, such as facts about the situation and options, and reasoning strategies that revolve around goals, options for action, and predictions about future outcomes.[11]

However, as we have seen, competition between automatic reactions and conscious processing can affect our judgment. Likewise, the tension between emotion and deliberation can affect the quality of our decisions. The challenge, then, is to organize our thinking and approach to making decisions in a way that is consistent with how we take in and process information and to leverage the multiple processes that contribute to our ability to reason and make choices and make them a positive force.

Two techniques help moderate the negative impact of our habits and assumptions and better balance reason and emotions to improve our decisions. They are (1) involving other people, which ensures we include perspectives and experiences other than our own and helps fill in relevant data we may not have, and (2) using a systematic process, which ensures we look at the relevant information and consider both the benefits and risks of each alternative.

Involve the Right People

Involving people in decisions helps tip the balance in favor of conscious processing and deliberation. It ensures we have access to information and perspectives that might not otherwise be available to us and decreases the likelihood that we will take action and make choices based solely on the familiarity of the situation ("I've seen this before and I know what needs to be done"). In addition, involving people increases decision acceptance, which is critical to effective execution once the decision has been made.

Victor Vroom, a professor and researcher at Yale University, and his colleagues Philip Yetton and Arthur G. Jago have conducted studies with over 100,000 managers to develop a model to help managers determine when and how to involve others in making decision.[12,13]

Over the years, various attempts have been made to simplify Vroom's model. In his book, *Skills for Managers and Leaders*, Gary Yukl, professor of management at the State University of New York in Albany, has developed a very accessible and useful version. Yukl describes three very different ways to involve people in making decisions.[14]

Autocratic Decision. With this approach you make the decision alone without asking direct reports or colleagues for their ideas and suggestions. Then you tell people what was decided and, if necessary, explain the decision or try to "sell" it to them.

Let's say, for example, that you're a production manager and one of your responsibilities is to order the materials used by your direct reports in production jobs. Extensive stockpiling of material is not feasible, and having idle workers due to lack of materials is costly. Based on past records, you have been able to determine with considerable accuracy which materials direct reports will need a few weeks in advance. The purchase orders are executed by the Purchasing Office, not by your direct reports.

In this situation an autocratic decision would be appropriate because you have all the information you need to make the best decision and the buy-in of your direct reports is not essential for execution.

Consultation Decision. With this approach you explain the decision problem to direct reports or colleagues and ask them for their ideas and suggestions. You may consult with people individually or together in a group. Then you make the final decision after careful consideration of their input.

For example, assume that you are the vice president for production in a small manufacturing company. Your plant is working close to capacity to fill current orders. Now you have just been offered a contract to manufacture components for a new customer. If the customer is pleased with the way you handle this order, additional orders are likely and the new customer could become one of your company's largest clients. You are confident that your production supervisors can handle the job, but it would impose a heavy burden on them in terms of rescheduling production, hiring extra workers, and working extra hours.

In this case consulting with your direct reports would be appropriate because you don't have all the information to make the best decision and you need the support and commitment of your direct reports to ensure effective execution.

Group Decision. Here you meet with direct reports or colleagues to discuss the decision problem and reach a decision that is acceptable to everyone, or at least to a majority of group members. Although you may run the meeting, you have no more influence over the final decision than any other group member.

Imagine that you have been appointed chairperson of a committee formed to coordinate the interdependent activities of several departments in the company. Coordination problems have interfered with the work flow, causing bottlenecks, delays, and wasted effort. These problems are complex and solving them requires knowledge of ongoing events in the different departments. Although you are the designated chairperson, you have no formal authority over the other members who are not your direct reports. You depend on committee members to return to their respective departments and implement the decisions made. You are glad that most members appear to be sincerely interested in improving coordination among departments.

A group decision would work in this situation because committee members share the same goals and you need a high level of commitment and support for effective execution.

As you can see, all three types of decisions are valid. The one you choose depends primarily on the unique set of circumstances surrounding the decision at hand.

From Vroom and Yukl's work we also know that the success of each type of decision depends primarily on three things: decision quality, decision acceptance, and the amount of time needed to make the decision.[15] Let's take a quick look at each.

Decision Quality. The quality of a decision is high when the selected alternative is the best one among those available. For example, an efficient work process is selected over an array of less efficient ones or a critical assignment is given to the most qualified person rather than to someone less qualified. Decision quality is important if the decision has significant consequences for the organization or group and some of the alternative choices are much better than others.

For most of your decisions, quality is likely to be important. However, no single decision procedure is always superior for making decisions when quality is important. What determines which procedure will be most appropriate? Mainly, it's the distribution of relevant information and the extent to which it is possible to bring this information to bear.

Not all decisions are created equal. For some decisions, all the obvious alternatives are equally desirable. For example, a manager may need to choose among three brands of supplies, all of which are comparable. In some cases the decision itself is a trivial one without serious consequences for the organization, like which brand of coffee to use in the office. In cases like this, when decision quality is not important, you obviously wouldn't agonize over selecting the right decision procedure.

In other cases, decision quality matters more. Consultation and group decision making will increase decision quality if the people who participate in the decision have the relevant information and problem-solving skills you lack and if they share your objectives. On the other hand, if you already have the information and expertise necessary to solve a problem or identify the best alternative, participative procedures will not improve decision quality.

How can you tell whether others have relevant information you need? This is likely the case if the decision has one or more of the following attributes:

- The cause of the problem is not obvious.
- There is no best solution, and any solution is likely to have some undesirable side-effects.
- Tradeoffs among benefits must be considered because more of one benefit means less of another.

Consider this example of Lynn, a department head with five section supervisors reporting to her. She has recently evaluated the present system for collecting and analyzing performance data on each section and found that improvements are needed. Some of her section supervisors complain that the present system fails to provide them with the kind of information they need to control their operations and plan effectively.

Lynn discussed the subject briefly with them and found that each section supervisor prefers a different kind of information or statistics on the daily reports. Yet none of the supervisors is willing to ask direct reports to fill out lengthy forms and reports.

Here, decision quality is important because the decision has consequences for the group's ability to do its job well. But it appears that the best alternative is not immediately obvious and the leader does not have all the information she needs to make the best decision. In addition, although some alternatives may be better than others, there are tradeoffs because any alternative may have an adverse effect on at least one of her departments.

Consultation and group decision making are equally effective for improving decision quality if you have the skills necessary to use the decision procedure effectively. These include the ability to keep the discussion on track, facilitate effective problem solving, and avoid problems such as hasty decisions for which the group fails to consider important information.

Decision Acceptance. The second requirement for a successful decision is the extent to which the people who must implement the decision believe in it and are motivated to overcome obstacles to make it work. Regardless of how good a decision is in terms of quality, apathy or resistance by the people who must implement it may cause it to fail.

Whether decision acceptance is important depends on the situation. Decision acceptance by others is not important if you will implement the decision yourself and it does not threaten the self-interest of other people. Autocratic decisions will most likely be accepted if you select an alternative that is favored by others, when others share your objectives and you are able to persuade others that your decision is the best way to achieve them, or when people believe you have the expertise to determine what is best.

Sometimes, it's obvious that an autocratic decision won't go over well. In such instances a participative approach is best.

Participative procedures increase acceptance because:

- When people have substantial influence over a decision, they tend to identify with it and assume ownership of it.
- By participating in making the decision, people gain a better understanding of the reasons for the decision.
- If people have an opportunity to express reservations about the possible adverse consequences of various alternatives, it's more likely that the final decision will deal with their concerns, thereby reducing resistance.
- When people make a decision using a process they feel is legitimate, the group is likely to use social pressure on any reluctant members to do their part.

If you were the manager of a production facility with four operating departments reporting to you, how should you make the following decision? The expense budget for your facility has just been reduced without any reduction in workload. Now you have to decide how much to cut each department's budget.

Not surprisingly, none of your department managers want to suffer a budget cut, and each believes that his or her department's activities should have the highest priority. On your own it's difficult to evaluate how budget cuts would affect each department's capacity to do its work because the evaluation requires more detailed information about the current operations of each.

Decision quality is clearly important, as a bad decision would have a detrimental effect on one or more of your departments' ability to do their work. Much of the information you need to make the best decision resides with your direct reports, and you need their support to effectively implement it. An autocratic decision about budget cuts would almost certainly result in a less-than-enthusiastic response from the members of your team—potentially setting you up for failure.

Decision Time. The third requirement for a successful decision is the swiftness with which it needs to be made. Naturally, decision time is most important in the face of a crisis that will grow worse if not dealt with quickly. However, even when there is not an immediate crisis, delays may entail direct costs and hard-to-measure lost opportunities.

Let's say, for instance, that you're a leader at a printing company and you need an expensive piece of equipment to ensure your products are as good or better than the competition. Dragging your feet on the buying decision could mean that you'll be left out of the running for lucrative retail holiday catalog contracts for customers you've been courting.

Furthermore, the time devoted to making a decision involves an overhead cost in terms of managerial person-hours and salaries. This cost escalates rapidly when many people spend hours in meetings aimed at making a decision.

The three decision procedures differ in the amount of time they require. Not surprisingly, autocratic decisions are usually the quickest. Group decisions require the most time, especially when the group is large or there is substantial conflict to be resolved. And the amount of time increases even more if the leader is looking for a consensus decision rather than a majority decision.

The Right Decision Style: Making Sense of All the Variables

Considering the relative importance of decision quality, acceptance, and time will help determine the most appropriate way to make the decision. The Decision Style Matrix presented in Table 5.2 gives highest priority to decision quality, second priority to ensuring acceptance, and lowest priority to saving time. Based on these assumptions, it shows each distinct decision situation and the most appropriate style to use in that situation.

Table 5.2 Decision Style Matrix

Decision Quality	Acceptance of the Decision	
	Not important, or assured with an autocratic decision	*Important, and not assured with an autocratic decision*
Not important (decision is trivial or there are many obvious good solutions)	Autocratic	Group
Important, but leader has sufficient information; members share leader's goals	Autocratic	Group
Important, but leader has sufficient information; members do not share leader's goals	Autocratic	Consultation
Important, and leader lacks essential information; members share leader's goals	Consultation	Group
Important, and leader lacks essential information; members do not share leader's goals	Consultation	Consultation

If your priorities are different—perhaps you feel that "time" is the most important consideration—it could result in a different recommended decision style.

Selecting the most appropriate decision style depends on your ability to assess a decision situation accurately. The guidelines in Table 5.3 will help facilitate that assessment.

The sequence of questions shown in Table 5.4 is an easy way to determine which decision approach is feasible and appropriate

Table 5.3 Diagnosing the Situation

Factors That Impact Decision Success	When the Factor Is Relevant
Decision quality is likely to be important if:	• The decision has important consequences for the organization or group • Some of the alternative choices are much better than others
Decision quality is not assured with an autocratic decision if:	• Direct reports or group members have relevant information and ideas needed by the leader to solve the problem • The decision problem is complex, and the best way to resolve the problem is not clear from the data or from prior experience with similar problems
Decision acceptance is likely to be important if:	• The leader must depend on direct reports or group members to implement the decision • Successful implementation requires a high degree of effort and initiative by direct reports or group members • Failure to gain acceptance would have unfavorable consequences for direct reports or group members
Decision acceptance is not assured with an autocratic decision if:	• The leader does not have enough personal power and influence over direct reports or group members to ensure their loyalty and support

Table 5.3 (*Continued*)

Factors That Impact Decision Success	*When the Factor Is Relevant*
	• Direct reports or group members are likely to resist any decision that is not consistent with their strong preferences in the matter, and the leader does not know what these preferences are • Direct reports or group members expect to participate in making the decision, and may resist even a decision consistent with their preferences if excluded from the decision process
Direct report or group member goals are not likely to be consistent with the leader's goals if:	• They prefer an alternative that is outside of the leader's range of acceptable options • They are known to be hostile or unsympathetic with regard to the leader's objectives • There is an obvious conflict of interest or difference in priorities between the leader and direct reports or group members

for a particular decision situation. These questions, along with the Decision Style Matrix, are two tools you can use to help you determine who and how to involve others in making decision.

When you first start using these tools, you may want to refer to them periodically to remind yourself what the next step or question should be. But after you've worked with them for a little while, you'll find you've internalized the questions and their sequence and that you're able to analyze a situation and determine the best approach "in the moment."

Table 5.4 Selecting a Decision Approach

Situational Factors	Yes	No
Is decision quality important?		
Does the leader have the information to make a high-quality decision without direct-report participation?		
Is decision acceptance important?		
Is acceptance assured with an autocratic decision?		
Do direct reports share the leader's task objectives?		

A Systematic Decision-Making Process Outsmarts the Brain

If you're not accustomed to using guideline questions and matrixes when making decisions, you're not alone. Most leaders probably use a more seat-of-the-pants or emotion-driven approach or base their decisions solely on history ("This is how I've always done it"). But as I've demonstrated in this chapter, you can't always rely on your own perceptions or feelings. Even if you're experienced and the most rational person in the world, your brain can steer you wrong.

Using an objective, systematic method for decision making can address many of the potential problems caused by how we take in and process information and make choices. It is a way to overcome our brain's more immediate tendency to make decisions based on past experience and it reduces the negative impact emotions can have on rational thought by ensuring there is more of a balance between the two.

A systematic approach also makes what is usually an internal thought process more explicit and ensures that the broad-based knowledge about each alternative is visible—which, in effect, provides a platform upon which our individual or team's reasoning strategies can more effectively operate.

The five-step approach described below reflects the work of Charles H. Kepner and Benjamin B. Tregoe, who developed a model of decision making based on the thought process used by effective decision-makers.[16] This type of structured formal process is most appropriate in situations when you have to justify your choice, when stakeholders have different priorities and objectives and conflicts need to be resolved, when you need to find the best option versus the first workable option, and when the situation is complex and the components are not easily recognized or analyzed.[17]

As you'll see below, the five steps are (1) developing a decision statement, (2) developing decision criteria, (3) comparing alternatives, (4) determining the risk of each alternative, and (5) making a choice. There are actually six steps because the first step is to ask: "Is the best alternative readily apparent?" If it is, just emulate the firefighter who immediately assessed the situation and knew based on his experience what needed to be done. Eschew the formal structured decision process and embrace your automatic reaction and you will likely be on target.

Step 1: Develop a Decision Statement. A clear, concise decision statement clarifies the purpose of the decision and focuses people's attention on specifically what they need to do. This is particularly helpful when those involved don't have a shared picture of the decision's purpose. The statement also acts as a check to ensure that the action you think should be taken is based on an accurate perception of the current situation and not on some previous experience that looks similar on the surface. Even for a less complex, straightforward choice, it helps to start by asking yourself, "What do I want to accomplish?"

The wording of the decision statement matters. Why? Because it defines the scope of the decision, affects the range of alternatives to consider, and drives the development of decision criteria. Let's say you need to make a decision on how you can get to work. A broad decision statement like "provide transportation to work" could include alternatives like public transportation, carpools, bicycle, car rentals, or car purchases. A narrower decision statement like "buy a car to drive to work" narrows the options available; basically, the only choices for consideration would be whether to buy a new or used car. The decision criteria would also be quite different for each of these decision statements.

Examples of good decision statements include:

- Select a strategy for increasing our market share of Product X.
- Choose a location for the new customer service center.
- Select a sales manager for the central region.
- Upgrade the voicemail system.

Step 2: Develop Decision Criteria. Decision criteria answer two questions: *What will the best alternative look like?* and *What are the constraints (such as cost, time, and resources)?* Developing decision criteria ensures you will assess the alternatives in an objective manner. It minimizes the likelihood of making a purely emotion-driven choice and it slows our automatic reaction, which gives our conscious processing a chance to be considered. However, the intent is not to eliminate emotional or experience considerations altogether. They will come into play but later in the decision process.

The decision criteria are made up of *screening* and *comparing* criteria. *Screening criteria* are the "musts" or required characteristics and are mandatory, quantifiable, and realistic: for instance, "costs less than $15,000" and "delivered in thirty days." An alternative must meet all screening criteria to remain under consideration, no exceptions. You should not set too many screening criteria because that may prematurely eliminate alternatives.

Comparing criteria describe the "wants" or desired characteristics. They help us choose among alternatives that meet all the screening criteria. Comparing criteria are more subjective and do not have to be measurable. Some comparing criteria are more important than others, so each is assigned a value from 1 through 10 (1 is least important, 10 is most important). Different criteria can have the same importance value. You can use the same criteria to both screen and compare alternatives by converting screening criteria into comparing alternatives. For example, "costs less than $15,000" could be converted to "minimum cost."

Exhibit 5.1 provides a worksheet that can be used to list your decision criteria and identify which is screening and which is comparing.

Exhibit 5.1 Establishing Criteria Worksheet

Decision Statement:	
Decision Criteria	Will This Be Used for "Screening" or "Comparing"
1.	
2.	
3.	
4.	
5.	
6.	
7.	

Step 3: Compare Alternatives. After clearly defining the decision statement and the screening and comparing criteria, you can start the work of evaluating each alternative. Exhibit 5.2

illustrates the process for capturing and evaluating the information for each alternative.

Charting a complex decision, or one where the best alternative is not apparent, has four benefits. First, it provides a catalyst for conversation and debate among participants, which increases the likelihood you will get everyone's best thinking. Second, it ensures everyone is working off the same information and facilitates memory storage.

Third, the focus on facts and data help minimize our tendency to over-emphasize emotion in the decision process. Emotion, opinion, experience, and preference come into play when we evaluate the more subjective comparing alternatives, but it is within a more controlled setting.

Fourth, by charting the data we can see where there are gaps in our knowledge. This enables us to target our search for information rather than embarking on the more time-consuming "see what else we can find out" kind of search.

The steps for comparing alternatives are

- Eliminate alternatives that don't meet all of the screening criteria.
  - Evaluate each alternative against each screening criterion.
  - Each alternative gets only a "Go" or "No Go" rating.
- Evaluate each remaining alternative ("Go") using the comparing criteria.
  - On a scale of 1 to 10, rate how well each alternative satisfies each comparing criterion.
    - Which satisfies it best? (Rate it as a 10.)
    - Relative to the alternative that you rated as 10, how well do the others satisfy that criterion?
    - Determine the total score for each remaining alternative.
    - Total score is a multiple of Value (of the comparing criterion) × Rating (of how well the alternative satisfies that criterion).
- Identify the highest-scoring alternatives.

Exhibit 5.2 Screening and Comparing Alternatives

Decision Criteria	Alternatives					
	A		B		C	
"Screening" Criteria	Information	Go/ No Go	Information	Go/ No Go	Information	Go/ No Go

Decision Criteria		Alternatives								
		A			B			C		
"Comparing" Criteria	Value (1–10)	Information	Rating (1–10)	Score	Information	Rating (1–10)	Score	Information	Rating (1–10)	Score
Total Score										

Remember, while a rating system can be very effective for complex decisions or when the perceived gain or loss is high, it might be overkill for the simpler decisions we make day-to-day. In these situations, it is still useful to develop a decision criteria so that you and everyone else involved are clear about what the best alternative needs to look like. The comparison, however, can be more of an informal discussion, without numerical ratings, that focuses on the relative merits of each option as it relates to the criteria.

A numerical rating can be very satisfying but, on its own, it is not enough to determine the best choice. In fact, it's not uncommon for more than one alternative to end up with the same total score or just a few points difference. The rating is only a reflection of the group's discussions and provides a sense of which alternative is preferred.

Plus, at this point in the game you've only looked at the positive side of the decision, the things you want the decision to accomplish or the parameters it must meet to be acceptable. Every decision has some risk associated with it, and you have not yet taken a close look at the downside risk associated with each alternative.

Step 4: Determine the Risk of Each Alternative. Many people tend to look at the upside of a decision without fully exploring the risks that come with it. This is a mistake. Our tolerance for risk should play a big role in determining which alternative we prefer, so Step 4 helps ensure we do not (a) unnecessarily avoid risk or (b) make a too-risky decision. Basically, identifying the potential risks or consequences associated with the alternatives you've tentatively selected means asking: "What could go wrong?"

Exhibit 5.3 illustrates the thought process behind risk assessment. Begin with the highest-scoring alternative and explore the potential downsides of each alternative. Start by listing everything you can think of that could go wrong and keep this alternative from being successful. Some of these potential problems may be things you overlooked when developing screening or comparing criteria. That's okay. Because the decision process is flexible, you now have a chance to go back and review the criteria and reevaluate the alternatives.

Assessing risk means looking into the future and anticipating what might go wrong. Because no one has a working crystal ball, this activity depends greatly on judgment and experience. This is another reason why it's important to involve the right people. To understand risks and potential downsides before making your final choice, you'll need to do three things:

- Forecast the probability of a situation or event occurring.
- Forecast the impact if it does occur.
- Determine how hard it would be to overcome the impact of the potential downside.

With the group's shared opinion of the probability and impact of each potential problem on full display, you can now lead a discussion on how to overcome potential difficulties to achieve the desired results. This discussion not only helps clarify the level of risk involved with each alternative but it also sets the stage for action planning.

Exhibit 5.3 Assessing Risk

H = High, M = Medium, L = Low

Alternative:			
Risk/"Downside"	Probability (H-M-L)	Impact (H-M-L)	Ability to Overcome (H-M-L)
1.			
2.			
3.			
4.			
5.			
6.			

Step 5: Make a Choice. Unfortunately, while this objective, systematic process gets you off to a good start, it does not actually make the decision for you. You must do that. If the alternative with the highest total score has unacceptable risk, consider the alternative with the next-highest score that has a more acceptable level of risk. The best choice will be the alternative with the best balance of risk and reward.

> That determination, however, does not jump out from the worksheets or conversations. Your judgment, experience, and how you feel about the option all play a part in the final decision. Your tolerance for risk will greatly affect your final choice. Now, however, your decision can be guided by both a rational assessment as well as experience, emotion, and feeling.

The Bottom Line

The brain is a complex organ, and decision making is a complex activity that uses many individual mental processes. In addition, many of these processes compete for dominance, and the quality of our decisions is determined by which ones win out. Awareness of this complexity and the many processes that are involved, in and of itself, increases the probability that you will monitor your reactions and choices to check that you are not just making choices based on a bias or taking a familiar action that has been reinforced by experience.

However, you can do three additional things to improve the quality of the decisions both you and members of your team make. First, make sure that people closest to the action are making the decisions. This can require a change in organizational structure and, when this is not possible, empowering people and holding them accountable for taking the initiative and addressing issues when they occur.

Second, involve the right people in decisions. This helps ensure that you include perspectives and experiences other than your own and also helps fill in relevant data that you might not possess.

Third, use an objective systematic process so that you won't let emotion or bias cloud the issues or simply default to the kinds of decisions you've made in the past. (This will also force you to incorporate risk assessment in your decision making.)

These last two actions ensure we have access to a range of perspectives and information that might not otherwise be available to us and increases the likelihood that we will be more thoughtful and rational when making choices.

Chapter Six

Bridge Builder 5: Facilitate Change Readiness

OnPoint Consulting's research on strategy execution identified ten factors that enable an organization to effectively execute initiatives and plans. The ability to manage change is one of these critical factors. (You may recall that it's the first of our "Five Bridges" that keep the strategy execution gap from forming—and enable a company to close it if it *does* form.) And it is a top priority on almost every list of organizational and leadership success factors.

Yet, despite the amount of time and money that have been invested in educating organizations and training leaders in the tools and skills to manage change, results have been uneven at best. The very public problems at General Motors, Home Depot, and Dell show that many organizations and leaders still struggle with change and managing it well.

Because it's such a critical component of execution, we wanted to zero in on what it takes to introduce and manage change effectively, what top-performing companies do well and where others fall short, and which leader behaviors have the greatest impact in reducing employee resistance and making change easier. And so we asked 655 middle- and senior-level leaders across industries to complete an online survey designed around these questions.[1]

Some of what we found did not surprise us. For instance, only 46 percent of leaders believe change is managed effectively in their companies and that their companies have good track records when it comes to introducing and managing change effectively.

Forty-three percent lack confidence that current organizational changes will be implemented effectively.

Some of the findings, however, *were* surprising. According to conventional wisdom, change is difficult to manage for several reasons: (a) entrenched workforces don't recognize the necessity of change, (b) employees generally fear change and prefer the status quo, and (c) change happens too quickly to be easily accommodated by employees. However, our survey results seemed to debunk all of these widely accepted beliefs.

It revealed (a) that 85 percent of respondents believe that their organizations must continue to change to grow and win in their respective industries, (b) that the majority of people (75 percent) report that they are comfortable with change and most (83 percent) believe a person can overcome his or her fears and get excited about change, and (c) that 41 percent believe that the pace of change in their organizations is "just right."

In other words, the poor track record many organizations have in managing change *cannot* be attributed to inflexible employees who prefer to maintain the status quo or who don't believe change is necessary for the continued growth and success of their organizations. Nor can the difficulties be attributed to the pace of change.

So what *does* account for the problems? I'll touch on some of these factors shortly. But first, let's take a look at how highly successful companies manage change.

What Top-Performing Companies Do

A client was telling me about the change initiative he was currently involved in and the challenges he faced. "You know," he said, "we've got a change architecture in place and we've made a convincing business case, but when it comes down to it you change an organization one person at a time."

Our findings support this observation. When you look at what the best companies do to prepare for and manage change,

you can clearly see that success hinges more on common
and leader behavior than on a change management structure
processes. Yes, there are plenty of change models available and,
although identifying change champions and sponsors and putting
an oversight committee structure in place is useful, it won't
eliminate the struggles that inevitably come with achieving our
change objectives.

Our research found that top-performing companies are more
effective at twelve common-sense practices critical to successful
change. These practices are outlined in Figure 6.1.

Figure 6.1 What Sets Apart the Best

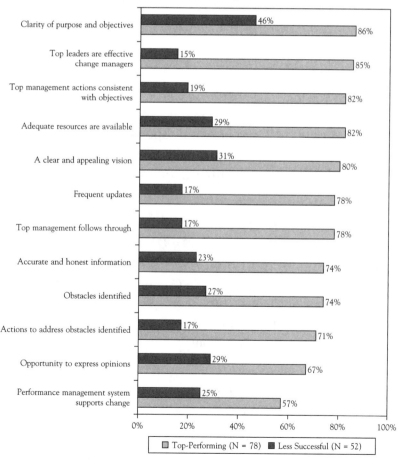

Practice	Top-Performing (N = 78)	Less Successful (N = 52)
Clarity of purpose and objectives	86%	46%
Top leaders are effective change managers	85%	15%
Top management actions consistent with objectives	82%	19%
Adequate resources are available	82%	29%
A clear and appealing vision	80%	31%
Frequent updates	78%	17%
Top management follows through	78%	17%
Accurate and honest information	74%	23%
Obstacles identified	74%	27%
Actions to address obstacles identified	71%	17%
Opportunity to express opinions	67%	29%
Performance management system supports change	57%	25%

☐ Top-Performing (N = 78) ■ Less Successful (N = 52)

hat these differentiators include some very
s:

nt updates

and honest information

- Providing opportunities for employees to express their opinions
- Making sure management actions are consistent with the objectives of the change initiative
- Identifying obstacles to implementation and actions to address these obstacles
- Ensuring that adequate resources are available
- Aligning the performance management system with the change

> When you look at what the best companies do, you see that change occurs through the direct interaction of a manager and his or her direct reports. It's not a sexy or glamorous process, but rather one that focuses on practical, fundamental management activities.

Three additional insights about how top-performing companies manage change came out of the study and can help guide what you do to increase the likelihood your change initiatives will be successful. These revolve around understanding the importance of the first three months of the change, engaging middle-level managers, and making sure employees don't lose their momentum and enthusiasm.

Stay Focused During the First Three Months . . . Success Depends on It

Many of the organizations in our survey try to apply commonly accepted guidelines for effective change management at the start of a change. However, there are significant differences in how well some companies are able to maintain people's support and commitment for the duration of the change initiative.

Top-performing companies appear to get off to a better start and have more favorable ratings for items such as *I understand why we need to change, The behaviors of top management are consistent with the objectives of the change,* and *I am willing to make personal sacrifices to help get the change implemented.* However, as things progress over the first three months, positive scores for many items related to support for, clarity about, and commitment to the change tend to decrease. And this is true for both top-performing and less-successful companies.

We will soon look at what causes this waning progress and commitment and what you can do about it. But, regardless of the cause managers at top-performing companies recognize what's happening and take action to reverse the trend sooner than in other organizations. As Figure 6.2 illustrates, top-performing companies are able to get back on track and stay there, while their less-successful counterparts take longer to reverse the trend—and even if they are able to do so, many times this reversal does not stick.

This trend highlights the critical nature of the first months of a change. The point is clear: things will almost certainly get

Figure 6.2 Trends Over Time: The Best Versus the Rest

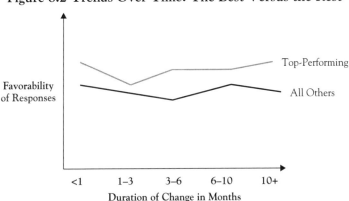

worse before they get better (even if you did everything right at the start) and if you don't take corrective action to get the change initiative back on track in the first one to three months, there is little likelihood that you'll fully achieve the objectives or realize its full potential.

Don't Just Focus on Senior Leaders . . . Involve Middle Managers and Keep Them Engaged

Academics, consultants, and internal change managers continually remind us that for a change to be successful you've got to get managers at all levels on board and engaged. But it appears this message has only been partially internalized in many companies. Senior-level respondents in our survey rated the following items significantly higher than mid-level respondents: *I have opportunities to express my concerns about the change, My concerns are taken into consideration when decisions related to the change are made,* and *I am involved in change-related decisions that affect me.*

> Unfortunately, as important as senior-level managers are to the success of a large-scale change initiative, it's usually the middle managers who do the heavy lifting and drive day-to-day execution. They are the ones who translate broad change objectives into specific actions for their team and its members. They are the ones who ensure that clear and consistent messages about the change and its progress are delivered to the general employee population. When they are on board and part of the process, middle managers help drive change and increase the likelihood of success. When they are not, they can be change-delaying bottlenecks.

So where are middle managers in terms of being involved and engaged in change? We found that in both the top-performing

Figure 6.3 Trends Over Time: Mid-Level Manager Involvement

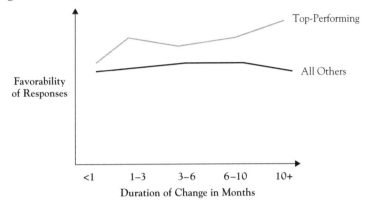

and the less-successful organizations, the level of mid-level-manager involvement is similar at the initiation of change. However, the top-performing organizations are more effective at maintaining and increasing the involvement of mid-level managers in the first three months than are the latter.

As shown in Figure 6.3, at the one-to-three-month mark top-performing companies experience a sharp increase in middle managers' mean scores on all three items mentioned above, while the less-successful companies remain fairly constant over time, with a slight drop-off at the ten-plus-month mark.

While this trend could be attributed to top-performing companies starting with an "advantage"—in other words, mid-level managers at less-successful companies might be more disgruntled at the start—this does not appear to be the case. Both top-performing and less-successful companies start with similar levels of involvement among mid-level managers.

Take Aggressive Action to Avoid the Commitment Dip

What can you do to avoid the decrease in support, the softening of employee commitment, and the loss of momentum that seem to occur during change? Quite a bit, actually. Based on our research, we identified ten guidelines—the "Do's" and "Don'ts" shown in Table 6.1—to help you avoid the dip in employee support and

Table 6.1 Avoiding the Commitment Dip

Do	Don't
Make sure leaders at all levels are involved and aligned right from the start; provide support to help senior leaders enlist their direct reports	Just focus on senior leaders
Hold everyone accountable for behaviors that support the change; make the clichés real—"walk the talk" and "practice what you preach"	Allow senior managers to revert to "old" behaviors or follow a set of "rules" that only apply to them
Continue frequent and honest communication for the duration of the change; be accessible and engage in "change talk" even when you don't have all the information	Take progress for granted and assume that once people are on board they will not reevaluate their commitment periodically
Maintain enthusiasm and excitement for the change; continue to celebrate successes and communicate benefit	Take momentum for granted and assume people will maintain high levels of morale and performance
Be realistic about what can be accomplished in the time available; set realistic goals and milestones	Over-promise
Prioritize change initiatives	Over-commit your resources
Anticipate the resources needed for the duration of the change	Overextend your resources
Frequently revisit and revise the plan	Put the plan on "automatic pilot"
Look for obstacles that may become apparent during implementation	Assume all obstacles and appropriate actions have been identified during the planning stage
Maintain focus on change objectives and expected outcomes	Let "squeaky wheels" or "new" challenges distract your attention or decrease your commitment

commitment and maintain positive momentum for the duration of the change.

Knowing how top-performing companies approach change management can be highly valuable. It provides a solid basis on which to improve the way you manage change. Yet, it's only a starting point. If you believe that change is managed one person at a time, you will need additional tools and techniques to facilitate individual and team readiness for change and to ensure that people are using behaviors that support the change objectives.

One very helpful, if somewhat unexpected, place to look for these tools is in the therapeutic work being done with people who are trying to change addictive behaviors like smoking, overeating, overdrinking, and drug abuse.

Kicking Old Habits: What Addicts Can Teach Us About Change

No doubt about it: change can be difficult. And no one knows that better than people who struggle with strong chemical and emotional addictions (and, of course, those who live with them). And yet, addicts of every type—from smokers to alcoholics to drug users—do manage to break their old habits and replace them with healthier new ones.

The work being done with these people can teach us a lot about helping employees change their behavior. If there are techniques and models that can help people kick a heroin habit or stop smoking, then these same techniques and models should also enable us to help people change more benign behaviors in the workplace.

The work of James O. Prochaska from the Cancer Prevention Research Consortium of the University of Rhode Island, Carlo C. DiClemente of the University of Houston, and John C. Norcross of the University of Scranton, who looked at thousands of research participants who were attempting to change addictive behaviors with and without psychotherapy, is particularly revealing and useful.[2] Several relevant ideas come out of their research.

- Individuals who are trying to modify their behavior move through five stages from "no intent to change" to "maintenance." They also found that we do not jump from "no intent to change" to "taking action" on the way to maintenance. We must move through each of the five stages in order to achieve sustainable behavior change.

- A set of specific strategies can be used to facilitate the shifts from one stage of change to the next, but Prochaska found that effective change in behavior only results when the right strategies are used at the right time. For example, an intensive action-oriented smoking cessation program was very successful for people who were in the "action" stage but very unsuccessful for people in the "contemplative" stage.

- Change is not a linear process and most people do not maintain the change in behavior on their first attempt. People will recycle through the stages several times before the new behavior is a habit. For example, many people report four or five years of making the same New Year's resolution before maintaining the behavior change for six months.

The Five Levels of Change Readiness

Bruce Fern and Herb Cohen of Performance Connections International have taken Prochaska's work and adapted it to a business environment. "We were unsatisfied with traditional change management models because they espouse a one-size-fits-all approach to behavior change," said Fern. "That's why we were excited to discover a well-researched and validated model that supports our belief that people don't just leap from an old behavior to a new behavior and that provides guidelines that help you tailor your approach to change based on the readiness and needs of the other person."

The five levels of change readiness are summarized in Table 6.2.

Level 1: Zero Intent to Change

As the name implies, this is the stage at which there is no intent to change in the near future. Indeed, many people at this stage are unaware of the need to change. A comment attributed to

Table 6.2 The Change-Ready Model

Level	Description	Evidence	Commitment
1. Zero Intent to Change	No intent to adopt a new behavior	No sign of the behavior	None
2. Contemplating Change	Considers using the behavior, but have not decided to yet	No use of behavior, but less open resistance	Low to none
3. Planning and Preparation	Getting ready, preparing, planning to change behavior	Thinking about it, talking about "how to" with others	Present, but not visible
4. Visible Action	Demonstrates the behavior, but not consistently	Observed use of behaviors, but variable and can slip back	High, but can waver
5. Habit	Behavior is now second-nature	Consistent use of behaviors	Resolved and permanent

writer A. K. Chesterson captures the tone of this stage, "It's not that they can't see the solution. It's that they can't see the problem." Resistance to recognizing a need to change or to modify a behavior is the hallmark of this stage.[3]

Level 2: Considering Change

This is where people are aware of the need for change and are seriously considering it but have not made a commitment to action. They know what they want to do and where they need to go, but they are just not ready yet. People can get stuck in this stage for long periods of time. In one study, a group of two hundred smokers remained in the contemplating stage for two years and never moved to significant action.[4] People at this stage weigh the pros and cons of making the change and struggle with the positive aspects of staying the same and the costs of changing.

Level 3: Planning and Preparation

People in this stage intend to take action soon and may have even tried to change their behavior in the recent past. It is not wise to cut short the time spent in this stage because carefully thinking through how you will make the change and maintain the behavior increases your likelihood of success.[5] At this level people may demonstrate some small behavioral changes but they have not yet reached the point at which they are willing to go all the way. For example, smokers may smoke five cigarettes less a day or put off the first cigarette of the day by thirty minutes.

Level 4: Visible Progress

This is the stage where a person demonstrates the desired behavior. It involves the most overt behavior change and requires considerable commitment. This stage does not constitute actual change, though people often mistakenly think it does. Thus, they overlook the necessary work required to keep people at this stage and get them to maintain the change in behavior.[6]

Level 5: Habit

At this stage people have fully internalized the importance of changing their behavior and have confidence in their ability to effectively use the new habit. At this point the new behavior does not require a great deal of conscious thought. It has become second-nature and has replaced the old behavior.

Moving on Up: Facilitating Change with Level-Appropriate Strategies

To manage change effectively, you must be able to recognize each employee's level of change readiness, then use specific strategies to accelerate it. You can assess a person's level of readiness by judging what he says about the specific behavior change (don't mistake problem-solving language for resistance), his degree of candor with you (do everything possible to encourage openness), and his actions (don't mistake inconsistency as resistance—it might just be a sign that the person is at Level 4).

"The strategies are powerful, researched, and tested ways of accelerating the readiness to engage in new behaviors," says Fern. "Prochaska, Norcross, and DiClemente did a remarkable job of mapping specific strategies to the precise levels of readiness."

The change ready strategies will help you more quickly and easily move others through the levels of change and encourage them to adopt new behaviors consistent with your vision or business objectives. Table 6.3 shows how the strategies align with each level of readiness.[7]

Level 1 → Level 2: Moving from "No Intent to Change" to "Considering Change"

People at Level 1 deny or minimize the need for change. They may also fear the unknown and have concerns about failing. At this stage the objective is to get these people unstuck. As we will see later in this chapter, the more you tell someone why she

Table 6.3 Change-Ready Selection Tool

Objective: To help you select the optimal strategy to accelerate the readiness to change behavior.

Strategy	1. Zero Intent	2. Contemplate Change	3. Planning and Preparation	4. Visible Actions	5. Habit
Provide Knowledge and Feedback	→				
Explore Alternatives and Options	→	→	→		
Leverage Emotional Energy			→		
Compare to Self-Image		→			
Ask for Commitment			→	→	
Administer Rewards				→	
Restructure the Environment				→	
Enlist Helpers				→	

should change and how easy it is to make the change, the more stridently she defends her current point of view. Paradoxically, "preaching" about the benefits of change actually works against you at this point.

Actions that make people aware of their defensiveness and the impact of continuing to use the old behavior or not using the new behavior are much more effective in getting people to think about changing. Providing knowledge and feedback and exploring alternatives and options are two strategies that are most appropriate at this level. Let's explore them a bit further.

Provide Knowledge and Feedback. This strategy involves sharing information with the individual or team about the impact of using and not using the behavior, providing feedback and increasing their awareness of the personal use of (or lack of use of) the targeted behaviors, and using facts, data, and other people's input to help increase the desire to change.

Example: Several members of a tech support team have a tendency to be impatient with callers who are not technically skilled, often becoming abrupt with them. Their manager has them listen to recordings of their calls and discusses the impact on the customer. This helps them realize their behavior is inappropriate and may cause the customer to look for another provider. It also makes them ready to think about changing their behavior—which is a move into Level 2.

Hands-On Tools

- Give non-judgmental feedback on the lack of use of the desired behavior and the impact of that behavior.
- Help people become aware of the defensive statements they make when talking about the change—statements that may take the form of denial and rationalization.
- Help people analyze why they are hesitant to adopt the new behaviors.
- Provide articles or other information about the value of the targeted behaviors and the consequences of not changing.
- Don't nag, don't give up, don't support avoidance.

Explore Alternatives and Options. This strategy focuses on helping the individual or team realize that there are different ways to handle the situations they have to deal with and on expanding their understanding of their options and choices in these situations (such as different ways to engage in the targeted behaviors).

Example: Colleen, a manager, is overwhelmed with her workload and feels she does not have the time for one-on-ones with her staff. Instead of meeting each week for an hour with each person, as she has traditionally done, Colleen's boss suggests she meet with them once every two weeks, either over lunch or early in the morning. This idea seems doable to her and she considers it seriously.

Hands-On Tools

- Brainstorm alternate, more appealing ways to engage in the targeted behavior.
- Help people identify the pros and cons of using and not using the targeted behavior.
- Discuss different options for compliance.
- Have the person observe and talk to others who already use the targeted behaviors.
- Give people an opportunity to discuss their beliefs about the situations that surround the targeted behaviors and the use of the behaviors themselves.
- Arrange for the person to spend less time with people who are "anti-change."

Level 2 → Level 3: Moving from "Contemplating Change" to "Planning and Preparation"

At Level 2 people have moved out of avoidance mode and are ready to talk about the change. They begin to focus more on the future. While they recognize that changing their behavior has some advantages, they are far from actually making a commitment. They continue to wrestle with the pros and cons of making the change. Many people can get stuck at this level for a long time, and your objective is to help them move from contemplation to planning for action. The two strategies that can help you accomplish that objective are leveraging peoples' emotional energy and comparing their current behavior to their self-images.

Leverage Emotional Energy. This strategy involves leveraging any distress or other strong emotions the individual or team may have to help them increase their desire to change—and to help them think deeply about the consequences of not doing so.

Example: Allison, a supervisor, is very responsive when she is told what to do, but does not otherwise take initiative to take action on her own. She gets a low performance review on this aspect of her performance. Her mentor points out that not being a "self-starter" will likely prevent her from advancing through the ranks at her company. Allison knows it is true and is a little disgusted with herself about her lack of proactive behavior.

Her mentor sees that Allison is upset about the feedback and says, "I understand you are disappointed in yourself and see this as a derailer. But you've overcome other leadership challenges and I believe you can do it again." In this way the mentor encourages Allison to use her feelings to motivate her to change rather than getting defensive.

Hands-On Tools

- Identify and discuss the benefits of the new behavior for the person, colleagues, and the company.
- Help the person or team see how not using the targeted behavior causes problems for others.
- Leverage emotionally charged events and personal experiences (such as a failure, heated argument with

someone else, or complaints about them) as the catalyst to adopt the new behavior.

- Don't minimize any negative feelings about not changing. Use those feelings to help increase the motivation to change.

Compare Current Behavior to Self-Image. The intent of this strategy is to help the individual think about how the targeted behavior is compatible with his desired self-image. Pose the question, "How do you want others to see you?" or "How do you want to see yourself?" and ask how the behavior fits that picture. Urge the person to think about the image he or she wants to project and compare the change being considered to that image. Ask, also, how *not* changing relates to that image.

Example: When Harold, a manager, hears about a problem from one of his direct reports, he gets visibly upset and critical. As a result, people avoid coming to him with problems. His boss asks him to think about the leadership image he wants to project—Does he *really* want to be known as Hair-Trigger Harold?—and he realizes that his reaction is inconsistent with the way he wants his direct reports to see him.

Hands-On Tools

- Discuss how the person wants to be perceived by others in the organization, and then compare the targeted behavior (or avoidance of that behavior) to those perceptions.
- Help him evaluate what he might lose and gain by engaging in the targeted behaviors and how that relates to his self-image.
- Help him clarify the pros and cons of changing in terms of the impact on his self-image and how others perceive him.
- Discuss the individual's values and clarify how the targeted behavior (or avoidance of that behavior) supports (or is inconsistent with) those values.

Level 3 → Level 4: Moving from "Planning and Preparation" to "Visible Progress"

Most people in the planning and preparation stage are making final adjustments before they begin to change their behavior. Often they appear ready to change, but they may not have fully resolved their ambivalence and may need to convince themselves to make the leap. Essentially, their awareness is high and they are on the cusp of action. At this point asking people to make a verbal commitment (either to you or to the team) about their intent can be enough to move them to action.

Ask for Commitment to Change Behavior. To reference the oft-quoted Nike slogan, ask the individual or team to "just do it."

Example: A company's account executives have been told to use a new, automated sales scheduling and tracking system. They have been hesitant to use the system because it is different and will take time to learn. In a series of one-on-one meetings, the senior sales executive asks each account executive to make a personal commitment to start using it next month.

Hands-On Tools

- Ask for a verbal commitment to change and to make the change a priority.
- Ask the person to make a public statement at a team meeting about his or her intent to change behavior.
- Divide the targeted behavior into small steps and ask people to commit to each step one at a time.
- Have the person commit to a specific time to start using the new behavior.
- Help the person acknowledge and work through any concerns about making the change successfully.

Level 4 → Level 5: Moving from "Visible Progress" to "Habit"

When we see visible action, we are inclined to equate it with actual behavior change. Because of this misconception, support for changers often dwindles when it's most needed. There is still plenty of work to do to ensure that people are able to consistently use the new behavior. The strategies that are most appropriate at this stage reinforce behavior and include administering rewards, restructuring the environment, and enlisting helpers.

Administer Rewards. This strategy focuses on providing positive reinforcement for desired behaviors and encouraging others to reward themselves after engaging in the targeted behaviors.

Example: The customer service reps who needed to start making sales calls have been doing it, but not consistently. Their manager makes a deal with them that if they make the required number of calls four weeks in a row they will get off early the next Friday.

Hands-On Tools

- Verbally recognize and reinforce visible demonstrations of the targeted behaviors.
- Reinforce gradual progress; provide praise and recognition for incremental steps toward the full completion of the targeted behavior.
- Leverage existing reward systems to recognize the use of the targeted behavior.
- Focus more on rewards and positive feedback, rather than on consequences and negative feedback to shape behavior.
- As the behavior becomes more common, reduce the rewards over time.

Restructure the Environment. To ensure that people do not revert to their old behaviors—and to make it easier to continue to use the new ones—this strategy focuses on changing elements of the environment. The idea is to infuse their world with reminders, supporters, and reinforcers for making the new, targeted behavior a habit.

Example: Two teams located in two different buildings do not keep each other well-informed about key issues. In order to improve communications, the director decides to move both teams onto the same floor in the same building.

Hands-On Tools

- Identify and adjust any aspects of the job or organization that get in the way of the fulfillment of the targeted behavior.
- Make sure people have the proper equipment and physical resources to perform the targeted behavior.
- Identify obstacles to task performance and remove them.
- Help people manage their daily and weekly schedules and workloads to support the performance of the targeted behavior.
- Have people identify when they need help getting work done so they can avoid slipping back to the old behavior and continue to use the targeted behavior.
- Ask whether people need help with anything that is out of their control that gets in the way of changing.

Enlist Helpers. Getting the help and support of others is crucial at this stage. That's why it's essential to encourage the individual or team to seek the assistance of others in order to permanently change their behavior. Helpers can be used in any stage of the behavior change process and the Visible Progress to Habit stage is no exception. Yet, too often, they are considered unnecessary at the later readiness levels. This is unfortunate because, in some ways, they are the most important at these higher levels, which hold the greatest risk of relapse.

Example: Thomas, a senior executive, wants to change the way he works with other people. He joins an executive peer coaching group that meets once a month and brings his behavior change goals to this group for ongoing support.

Hands-On Tools

- Identify people you trust and who are effectively using the new behavior to give you feedback on *your* use of it.
- Rehearse new behaviors with your trusted advisor.
- Ask helpers to be both patient and persistent.
- Encourage the use of multiple helpers and coordinate how they are working together.

Although these change ready strategies will help move people through the levels of change, they don't work in a vacuum. They require you, the leader, to behave in a way that supports and encourages others to change. How you approach and interact with people at each level of readiness will have a tremendous impact on the extent to which they will be open and receptive to your efforts.

Holding Up the Mirror: Understanding the Impact of Leader Behavior

Many of us try to get people to change behavior by asserting our view and trying to talk the person out of his or her viewpoint. This approach doesn't work.

Experiments conducted by Gerald R. Patterson and Marion S. Forgatch of the Oregon Social Learning Center, in which they looked at the impact of the therapist's behavior on the level of client resistance, prove the point.

The subjects of the studies were families who were referred to the therapists because of child management problems. The treatment calls for providing parents with a set of methods for altering both the pro- and anti-social behavior of the child—methods which require that the parents alter their reactions to the child and his or her siblings.

The sessions were videotaped and the therapist's behavior and the client's behavior were scored by different people. This analytic process allowed the researchers to identify moment by moment what one person did that impacted the behavior of the other. The study found that, when the therapist used "push" behaviors like "lecture" or "tell" and "confront," it elicited a significant increase in client resistance, while "pull" behaviors such as "facilitate" or "ask" and "support" were followed by a decease in client resistance.[8]

Patterson also observed that the interaction between the therapist's behavior and the client's reaction to that behavior created a kind of self-fulfilling prophecy. As the therapist continued to use "lecture" and "confront" behaviors, and as the client continued to resist, the therapist came to see the client in a negative way. It appears that when the therapist assumed the client would resist change and that confronting him was necessary to gain his compliance, the client reacted by digging in his heels—which then confirmed the therapist's initial assumption.

This is somewhat ironic. Because the therapists expected a certain behavior from the clients, they approached the clients in a way that caused the clients to behave exactly as they expected them to.

It's this aspect of the study—the role the therapist plays in the client's willingness to change—that I find most interesting. Direct argument, it appears, causes the other person to more vigorously support his or her position, which further entrenches his or her behavior pattern. A reflective and empathetic style, rather than an authoritative one, seems to be the most effective approach when we want someone to change behavior.[9]

The Importance of Change Talk

William R. Miller from the University of New Mexico in Albuquerque and Stephen Rollnick from the University of Wales in the United Kingdom found that ambivalence is the primary obstacle to change. People tend to feel two seemingly contradictory ways about making a change; they want to and they don't want to.[10] This is also known as the approach/avoidance conflict. And, as we saw from the work of Patterson and Forgatch, the tendency to make pro-change arguments only invokes the opposite side of this inner debate.

To help people deal with their ambivalence and resolve it in a positive direction, Miller developed a technique called Motivational Interviewing (MI). This technique encourages the person considering making a change to make the arguments for change herself (rather than having someone else try to convince her). Miller and Rollnick refer to this self-persuasive dialogue as "change talk."

To better understand why change talk was able to facilitate change readiness, they collaborated with Dr. Paul Amhein to analyze hundreds of MI sessions. They identified four patterns of speech and found that, when people were allowed to talk about their confidence in their ability to change, their desire to change, the importance of change, and their reasons to change, they were more likely to achieve the "Planning and Preparation" level on the Change Readiness Scale.

They also found that, by reinforcing change talk and commitment language, MI counselors were able to shape client speech so that it echoed the desired outcome—and this verbalization is what triggered behavior change.[11]

Bruce Fern of Performance Connections International has translated Miller and Rollnick's change talk theory into tools that can be used to facilitate change in the workplace. At work, change talk enables us to engage members of our teams in discussions that might otherwise be difficult to initiate or sustain. It provides us with a mechanism to evaluate people's level of change-readiness, clarify key issues, and begin the process of reducing resistance. Finally, it facilitates the move from one level of readiness to change to the next.

Change talk techniques include identifying the behavior the person or team needs to change, building trust, exploring importance and confidence, and conducting a pro/con analysis.[12]

Identify the Target Behavior

> If you can't name the behavior you want from people, you're unlikely to get the change you need. An inability to clearly indicate the specific behavior people need to change results in an inability to effectively communicate your expectations.

It's relatively easy to set a goal and expect people to follow through on those goals. However, many managers fail to take the next step of translating goals into behaviors to ensure everyone knows what they need to do in order to achieve the goal. For example:

Goal: Focus on higher-margin products.

Measurable behavior: Ensure each region makes fifty sales calls per month looking for needs related to higher-margin products.

Goal: Improve our collaboration with our strategic partner.

Measurable behavior: Set up weekly conference calls to check on progress per our strategic partnership plan.

Goal: Educate our clients about the new product.

Measurable behavior: Send new product brochures to all of our clients and follow up with a phone call to each within five days.

As we saw with the change-ready strategy of "Explore Alternatives and Options," the more a person feels that he or she has options, the greater the readiness to change. Therefore, it often helps to present the targeted behavior change in general terms at first and then work with people to identify options on how to implement it.

Let's say, for example, that the general behavior change is that the service team will have to start making sales calls. First, you tell them that this needs to happen. Then they can work with you on their options concerning how many calls per day to make, which days to make them on, what times of the day to make them, and so on.

Work to Build Trust

Carl Rogers reasoned that a lack of acceptance inhibits change and that feeling accepted frees us up to change. Trust lies at the center of this paradox. Your ability to facilitate behavior change in others is proportional to your ability to demonstrate acceptance, and thereby build trust with them.

Sometimes your perspective as a leader makes it difficult to understand why people feel and react the way they do. But by demonstrating acceptance you communicate your belief that everyone's perspective is valid from his or her point of view and that, with the proper support, he or she will be willing to accept the need for change.

Empathy is a way of showing you understand what others think and how they feel about the change. Figure 6.4 shows the relationship between the amount of empathy you exhibit and the degree of trust that results.

Figure 6.4 Empathy and Trust

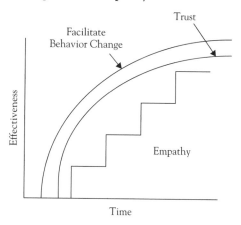

Reflective listening is the best way to show acceptance and empathy. It helps you overcome the natural instinct to debate with people who are being resistant. (Research clearly shows that the "Yes, but" response only increases resistance.) Reflective listening allows you to really understand the other person's point of view while still focusing on your change objectives. It shows that you hear and understand what the other person is saying without necessarily agreeing or disagreeing with his or her perspective.

It's easy to see how reflective listening enables you to build trust. It allows you to demonstrate that you are listening, defuse any negative emotions the other person may have, encourage him or her to explore the pros and cons of a specific behavior change, and avoid your own pressured reactions.

Reflective listening is demonstrated by paraphrasing what the other person said, using your own words, and reflecting any feelings attached to the message. For example:

Employee: "You want us to begin having user meetings once a week. This is just a waste of time and will lead to more problems and complaints."

Manager: "It sounds like you have some doubts about whether these meetings will be worth the time we will have to spend on them and that they may even make things worse."

Employee: "Exactly."

Particularly when they are upset or under stress, people will sometimes say things that can push your buttons and make you angry. They might criticize you, express a negative opinion about the situation, or say something disrespectful. Alternately, they might come across as unreasonably demanding, abrupt and curt, unresponsive to your requests, or self-serving. In any of these circumstances, it is important to keep your cool, and a great way of doing that is to paraphrase what the other person says.

> Why does reflective listening help you stay calm? First, it forces you to tune into the other person in order to paraphrase effectively. It also helps you calm the other person down which, in turn, will help you stay calm. And because it non-judgmentally reflects back what the other person is saying, it often leads him to retract or soften his position.

After demonstrating acceptance and empathy for the other person's viewpoint, most of us transition to making our points by saying something like, "Your points about not having user meetings make a lot of sense, **but** we still need to find better ways of communicating with our users." Guess what? The minute you say the word "but," you erase the empathetic statement and signal to the other person that you will be moving into a disagreement and argument mode.

Fortunately, there's a very easy way to avoid the "but" problem: just replace it with the word "and." Try saying, "Your points about not having user meetings make a lot of sense, **and** we still need to find better ways of communicating with our users." It's amazing how changing one simple word changes the tone of the entire statement.

Explore Issues of Importance and Confidence

As Miller and Rollnick found, getting people to articulate the importance of a change and their confidence in their ability to make the change themselves increases the likelihood that resistance to the change will diminish. One way to accomplish this objective is by exploring two critical questions with the other person. Ask:

- On a scale from 1 to 10, how important do you think this change is?
- On a scale from 1 to 10, how confident are you that you can make this change successfully?

When the other person gives you her "importance number," instead of asking, "Why is the number not higher?" ask, "Why is the number not lower?" ("Why did you give it a 6 instead of a 4?") The idea is to use the person's answer and encourage them to expand on it to emphasize his or her awareness of the need for change. In this way you reinforce her acknowledgment of the importance of making the change.

Of course, your instinct will be to try to convince the person that the number should be higher. Instead, help her talk herself into the importance of making the change. You can do this by reinforcing statements that support behavior change. When the person describes the importance of making the change, reinforce the change-talk by:

- Pressing for specifics by asking her to elaborate and
- Reinforcing the positive change statements by agreeing with the person's insights and comments that support the change

For example:

Manager: "You've rated the importance of having your team make these calls a 6 on a scale of 10. Why didn't you rate it lower? What do you see as the potential advantages of making this change?"

Team Leader: "Well, they would make more money, and that's good."

Manager: (Press for specifics) "In what ways would that be good?"

Team Leader: "Well, we cut back on overtime and almost all of them could use some extra income. Another advantage is that these calls would break up their day."

Manager: (Press for specifics) "What do you mean?"

Team Leader: "Well, sometimes the work they do gets monotonous and these calls would give them something different to do."

Manager: (Reinforce) "Yes, you're right that the extra income would be very nice for them, and that these calls will make their jobs more interesting."

Team Leader: "Yes, but I'm worried about their workload, and also how effective they'll be at selling."

If you're the manager in this scenario, you need to be careful how you react to the team leader's last comment. This is not necessarily an indication of continued resistance. It could also be a signal that she is ready to move to the Planning and Preparation level of readiness. In this case you could use a question like, "What are your ideas to address those issues?" Or you could suggest looking into these issues more closely as a way to transition to the Planning and Preparation level.

Next comes the confidence question. When the person rates her confidence in her ability to make the change, take the same approach you did with the "importance" question. However, rather than asking, "Why is the number not lower?" ask, "Why is the number not higher?"

Research shows that one of the reasons people fail to make a behavior change is their apprehension about making the change successfully. Your goal is to build the person's confidence in her ability to make the change. And, just like you did with the importance question, use reinforcing statements—press for specifics and reinforce positive change statements—to support the change talk. By encouraging her to focus on and discuss the areas in which she feels competent, you can help her see that she does have the capability to make the necessary change.

Another way to build confidence is to use the "looking back" technique. Ask the person or team to look back at a similar change he or she made in the past. Ask him to think about how he felt when first confronted with the need to change, how he got over that feeling, and how he made the change successfully. Generally, you'll find that the individual or team's confidence based on past victories gets transferred (at least in part) to the change at hand.

Conduct a Pro/Con Analysis

As we learned from the work of Miller and Rollnick, individuals and teams at the lower levels of readiness to change experience some form of approach/avoidance conflict (they want to change and they don't want to change). You can bring this to the surface by conducting a pro/con analysis of making the behavior change. The pro/con analysis, which is shown in Exhibit 6.1, helps the individual or team identify:

- The advantages of staying the same
- The disadvantages of staying the same
- The advantages of making the change
- The disadvantages of making the change

Exhibit 6.1 Pro/Con Analysis Worksheet

Describe the behavior:

Staying the Same		Behavior Change	
Advantages	*Disadvantages*	*Advantages*	*Disadvantages*

When discussing the advantages of changing, you again want to encourage and support change-talk by pressing for specifics and reinforcing positive change statements. As depicted in Figure 6.5, a well-researched observation by Miller and Rollnick is that the greater the weight others assign to the advantages of changing, the higher the level of readiness. As their perceptions of the weights change, so does their readiness to change.

Knowing this gives you a powerful metric for evaluating and measuring readiness. When others assign greater weight to the reasons for not changing, you know they are still in the lower levels of readiness. When they begin to assign greater weight to

Figure 6.5 Evolving Views of the Benefits of Changing as Readiness Increases

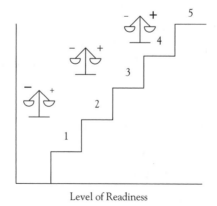

Level of Readiness

the reasons for changing, you know they are moving into the higher levels.

The Bottom Line

Execution, especially of large-scale strategic initiatives, frequently requires a change in behavior on the part of those who you depend on to successfully deliver the expected results. Most leaders would agree that change is ubiquitous and the need to effectively manage change is required if we want to get anything done. Yet, despite all the effort and resources that have been devoted to improving how well change is managed, managers and organizations still get poor marks in this area.

However, another change management process or program is probably not the solution. Change is made one person at a time, and our research, as well as the research of others, points to leader behavior as the key to effectively managing change.

Some of the most powerful tools and models for creating behavior change come from work being done with people trying to change addictive behaviors like smoking, overeating, and drug abuse. The lessons learned from this and other research—that leader behavior has a direct impact on the level of resistance demonstrated by the other person, that people are much less likely to successfully make a behavior change if they are forced to move to action before they are ready, and that there are specific strategies to help move people through the levels of change but they must be used a the right time—can guide our behavior and prescribe the actions we should take to facilitate change in others.

When people say that someone leads and manages change effectively, they specifically mean that they can observe consistency of that leader's actions and behavior with change objectives. It turns out that something as straightforward as modeling behaviors that facilitate change is the primary difference between the most effective change managers and those who are less effective.[13]

This core behavior goes beyond verbally endorsing a change. It is not enough to just say the right thing or even enthusiastically communicate the benefits and the business case for the change. Employees want to see those words backed up with behavior. That is how they judge how effectively someone is leading and managing a change.

This core behavior is exemplified by specific actions such as behaving in a way that is consistent with the change, doing what you say you will do related to the change, providing accurate and honest information about the change, being aligned with other managers around the need for change, and ensuring the timing of the change is realistic.

Chapter Seven

Bridge Builder 6: Increase Coordination and Cooperation

If you've ever worked in a public or private organization of any size, you know the truth: cooperation and coordination are critical to execution. It is almost impossible to get anything important done without the assistance and joint efforts of others. Yet, despite the fact that there's little argument about the role coordination and cooperation play in the execution of plans and initiatives, it appears that they are elusive and difficult to attain.

Only 56 percent of the managers who participated in our execution gap survey responded favorably to the question, "*Managers cooperate to achieve the objectives of the company rather than focusing on their own individual careers or work unit interests*" and even fewer, 49 percent, responded favorably to "*Decisions and actions are well coordinated across different work units and levels of management.*" If both are needed for success, the question is: Why is it difficult to get people to work together toward the same goals?

Cooperating Versus Competing: The Human Struggle

Are human beings naturally inclined to be cooperative or competitive? As with most matters of human behavior, the answers aren't always clear-cut. There is plenty of disagreement on the subject, and I will explore both sides in this chapter.

Economic and rational choice theories point to our competitive nature and a propensity to put our own self-interest ahead of the well-being of the group. Garrett Hardin was one of the first modern writers to describe this dilemma and its consequences in his classic article, "The Tragedy of the Commons." Hardin uses the analogy of a common pasture available to everyone to explain why our primary inclination is to maximize personal benefit.

Hardin starts with the observation that, as a rational being, each herdsman is motivated to keep as many head of cattle as possible on the common. This behavior isn't a problem until the time comes that the common can sustain only the existing number of cattle and each additional head of cattle results in overgrazing. At this point the rational herdsman would ask, "What's in it for me to add one more head of cattle to my herd?"

As he assesses the situation, the herdsman recognizes that on the positive side he would get all the proceeds from the sale of the additional cattle. On the negative side, there would be overgrazing by the additional animal that would eventually destroy the common. However, this negative effect would be shared by everyone and would have only a small effect on any one herdsman.

Looking at the cumulative effect of the positive and negative impact of his decision, the rational herdsman would conclude that the only sensible choice is to keep adding animals to his herd. Unfortunately, this behavior has a tragic outcome because every herdsman would make the same decision. All the herdsmen are locked into a system that motivates them to act in their own best self-interest until there is nothing left for anyone.[1]

How is this analogy relevant to today's world? Just look at the impact of self-interest in a modern day tragedy of the commons: the U.S. healthcare debate. Just like the herdsman in Hardin's analogy, the industry's key stakeholders—hospitals, doctors, pharmaceutical companies, and insurance companies—are all taking actions that benefit themselves but that will eventually undermine the overall system. It's not difficult to see how "rational" self-interest, and a lack of appreciation for how individual actions impact all participants, undermines cooperation and eventually destroys the "common."

Game theory also supports the hypothesis that self-interest undermines cooperation. The most famous example of this behavior is the Prisoner's Dilemma, a simple game that has been around since the 1950s and that illustrates the conflict between what is best for the individual and what is best from a collective point of view.

In the game two players have to decide (without any communication with each other) whether to cooperate or compete. If they both cooperate, each player gets 3 points. If they both defect (by choosing not to cooperate), each gets 1 point. But if one defects and the other cooperates the defecting player gets 5 points and the player who cooperated does not get any points.

In this situation, would you cooperate? It's a tough question. If you think it through carefully, you may well conclude that no matter what the other player does your best option is to defect. Chances are the other player, who is in the same position, will also defect—which means each player will only get 1 point. Why not cooperate? Because one "sure bet" point, coupled with the possibility of a whole lot more, is better than the very real likelihood of receiving nothing.

It's true that the reward when both players cooperate is greater than when both players defect, but a one-sided defection has an even greater temptation—a bigger reward than the reward for cooperation. In addition, each player may legitimately fear getting stuck with the "sucker's payoff" if the other player defects—which is even less than the "punishment" payoff when both players defect.

Clearly, based on these "rewards" and "punishments," your best move is to defect, which then leads to mutual defection.[2]

Of course, not everyone behaves the way economic and game theory models predict. In fact, there is evidence that people cooperate more often than theories of self-interest and maximizing personal benefit might suggest.

As we saw, in the one-round Prisoner's Dilemma the option to defect is always better than the option to cooperate. However, when the same individuals were allowed to interact multiple times, the results were often very different. Why? Because you think twice before defecting if your actions make your co-player think about defecting in the next round.[3]

> Many social scientists believe that cooperation may be society's more natural state.[4] This is because for much of our history we lived in hunter and gatherer societies, which tend to support cooperation for both efficiency and for maximizing individual good. Several cross-cultural studies showing that the degree of cooperation may be culturally driven support this position.

In *Cooperation and Competition Among Primitive People*, Margaret Mead describes several societies in which cooperation appears to be the dominant state. For example, the Arapesh of New Guinea is a society within which cooperation toward a shared goal is obtained through helpfulness in person-to-person relationships rather than by allegiance to a particular group or by resorting to rivalry or competition between groups. All economic activities are conducted in small groups, which work together based on personal ties between members and with little regard for formal clan structure.[5]

Another example is the Iroquois, whose society reflects the attitudes of women who are never involved in individualistic activities. Their activities coincide with cooperative and pacific principles, and the ritual of religious, civil, and mourning councils and the organization of ceremonial feasts constantly reiterate these cooperative principles.[6]

Additional support for the idea that we've developed an instinct toward cooperation over the centuries comes from neuroscience. When the brains of Prisoner's Dilemma players were scanned, researchers found that mutual cooperation activated brain areas associated with reward processing. This seems to imply that we perceive and react to acts of cooperation in a way that's similar to our perceptions and reactions when we receive a reward.[7]

J. Mark Weber's and J. Keith Murnighan's research on social benefit games—in which participants are asked to choose between actions that benefit themselves at the expense of the group and actions that benefit the group more than themselves—seem to point to this "instinct toward cooperation" as well. Weber and Murnighan discovered that, even when interactions are anonymous and there is no communication between players, people who were repeatedly cooperative in all situations still emerged among groups that participated.

This finding clearly shows that there are some people whose initial natural inclination is to cooperate and focus on the greater good of the group—even at the expense of greater personal benefit.[8]

Cooperation Is a Delicate State

Cooperation may be our natural inclination, but it is much more fragile than competition. John Monterosso and his colleagues conducted an interesting experiment where they tested the strength of mutual cooperation and mutual competition. Ninety subjects, participating in a multiple-round Prisoner's Dilemma game, were divided into two groups and permitted no communication. Subjects from one group were paired with someone from the other group and each sat at a computer on different floors of the building.

Both players had the same two options: If they chose Option 1 they received 100 points and the other player got nothing; if they chose Option 2 each player received 70 points. One person was randomly chosen to make the first move, and both players were told how much they earned at the end of each session.

Here's the interesting twist: whenever a pair of players reached a point of stable play, defined as ten consecutive choices of either defection or cooperation, false feedback was introduced to each player for eight rounds. It started with *false feedback* that was the *opposite* of whatever they were actually doing; that is, if the pair was cooperating, they each received feedback that the partner was defecting, and visa versa, although the other person's behavior had not changed. Then, after four rounds, it changed to recovery false feedback.

For example, if a pair had been cooperating for ten consecutive rounds, for the next four rounds each received false feedback that the partner was defecting. This was followed by four rounds of false feedback stating that the partner had resumed cooperating (even if he was actually defecting).

What Monterosso found explains a lot about why it is so difficult to establish long-term cooperative relationships. Although cooperation was initially a more common response, steady cooperation was more easily disrupted by false feedback of defection and it took longer to get back to cooperative interactions than it did to get back to competition.[9]

It seems that we are quicker to stop cooperating than we are to stop competing, and it takes longer for us to forgive and trust those who have defected in order to resume cooperating. If you think about similar situations in your own life, you'll probably agree with this assessment.

Encouraging and Sustaining Cooperation

With self-interest and the fragility of cooperation working against you, encouraging and sustaining cooperation and collaboration with people you depend on to get things done is a daunting challenge. However, it is not an insurmountable one. Certain conditions predict when cooperation is more likely to trump competition — namely, when communication is clear and there is transparency about intent, when people understand what they can expect from the other person and how they will work together, and when the interests of individuals or groups are aligned.

Let's discuss how to create these conditions in your company.

Cooperation Builder 1: Improve Communication and Transparency

An artificial element of the Prisoner's Dilemma is that players are not allowed to talk with each other. In the real world we often have an opportunity to communicate with people on whom we depend and, when we are given the chance to communicate our intent to cooperate, we can increase the likelihood the other person will respond in kind. This, of course, assumes that our communication is clear and our intentions are understood.

Two examples from Gary Klein's experience studying how people make decisions drive home the fact that we may not always be as clear as we think we are. During an operation a surgeon decided to lower the patient's blood pressure and tells the anesthesiologist to administer a drug to accomplish that objective. However, he did not tell the anesthesiologist why he was making the request.

The anesthesiologist's job is to maintain the patient's vital signs, so naturally when he saw the blood pressure drop he administered a drug to get it back to normal. Upon seeing a rise in blood pressure, the surgeon requested another dose of the first drug. The anesthesiologist complied with the request, and when he saw the pressure rise again he administered the drug to boost the pressure. Unfortunately, the lack of clear communication between the surgeon and the anesthesiologist went on until the patient died.[10]

Another example of poor communication that was not as tragic but still very dangerous involved a military flight crew. There was a leak in one of the fuel tanks located in the right wing and, although the captain was concerned about not being able to fly as far, he was more concerned about maintaining balance. To restore balance he instructed the flight engineer to reconfigure the flow of fuel so all engines were fed from the tanks in the left wing.

The flight engineer, however, either ignored or misunderstood the request. After all, his main responsibility was to manage the fuel flow and, because he didn't have to handle the controls, he was more concerned about a shortage of fuel. When the captain saw that the flight engineer had not carried out his request, he repeated it, and the flight engineer assured him that he would make sure they didn't waste any fuel.

After repeated attempts, and with the help of the co-pilot, the flight engineer finally understood what the captain was asking and complied with his request. When the plane landed there was an imbalance of two thousand pounds between the two wings—and the maximum imbalance for safe landing is one thousand pounds.[11]

In both situations people were acting with good intent and doing what they thought was right, but because communication was poor they were unable to cooperate and coordinate their actions. One cause was that both the captain and surgeon made the mistake of assuming the other person was able to read his mind and understand what he wanted or intended. The lesson for business professionals is simple: don't make that assumption. Develop the habit of being explicit about *why* you are doing something or making a request.

The second mistake was that no one in either of the scenarios—not the captain or the flight engineer or the surgeon or the anesthesiologist—bothered to do a "comprehension check." The flight engineer and the anesthesiologist both assumed they understood and did not repeat in their own words what the captain or surgeon had said to ensure what they were thinking was what the other person intended. And neither the captain nor the surgeon asked them to repeat back the directives.

The lesson is clear. Two simple actions—not assuming people know what you are thinking and paraphrasing to check for understanding—can go a long way toward making communication clear and transparent. These actions could have averted disaster (and near-disaster) in the scenarios above, and they can help prevent communication-related missteps in your own company as well.

Cooperation Builder 2: Agree on When Cooperation Is Needed and What It Looks Like

Lack of clarity about roles and responsibilities is another cooperation-crusher. It results in conflicts among team members or departments. It also allows key responsibilities to "fall through the cracks" because each party believes that someone else is responsible for them. It seems our level of cooperation is generally higher when everyone involved agrees on when it's needed and what it looks like in these situations. When we know what to expect from other people, we are more willing to trust them and take the risk of cooperation. Let's look at an example.

A U.S. based, wholly owned subsidiary of a Japanese pharmaceutical company found its growth objectives threatened because of role ambiguity and the resulting lack of cooperation and coordination among members of its R&D function. When the company was smaller, each therapeutic head had been able to carve out a comfortable niche for his or her area, a practice that continued as the company grew. Each manager acted as if his or her development projects had the highest priority.

Managers frequently ignored requests or decisions they disagreed with and seldom worked with colleagues to coordinate activities that required shared resources (such as clinical trials and the timing of regulatory submissions). As a result, many projects were behind schedule and the leaders in Japan were losing confidence in the teams' ability to deliver on their commitments.

Although individual conversations were held with each member of the R&D team to encourage more cooperation, there remained a fundamental difference of opinion about roles and who needed to be involved in key decisions. The solution? A meeting during which the team listed the decisions and activities for which they shared accountability. Using that list as a starting point, the team discussed and agreed on the level of authority and degree of involvement each person needed to have in order to ensure work was done efficiently, on time, and well.

The agreements were then documented and distributed to each manager's department so the behavior of direct reports would be consistent with the agreements reached by the managers.

The tool this R&D team used is shown in Exhibit 7.1 and is commonly referred to as the RACIN model. The tool, whose acronym stands for five levels of authority and involvement—*Responsible, Approve, Consult, Inform*, and *Not Involved*—enables individuals and teams to describe what cooperation and collaboration looks like for the most important decisions and activities for which they are responsible.

As we saw in the R&D team example, the team starts by listing the critical decisions and activities for which they are accountable and then discusses and reaches agreement on who has which role. The process takes time but it is well worth the investment. On their own, some teams may eventually come to an understanding about when and how to work together. That journey, however, takes much longer than a RACIN meeting and relationships and trust can be damaged along the way.

The reality is that, when left to its own devices, the team is likely to never reach a sustained level of cooperation, as its members repeatedly work through misunderstandings and conflicts. Formally and explicitly working out roles at the early stage of a team's formation, or whenever you notice a lack of cooperation and coordination, helps accelerate the process and preserve trust.

Exhibit 7.1 RACIN Model

Responsible

If a group or person is deemed "Responsible" for a decision or activity, he or she is charged with "making it happen." "R's" have the lead role in bringing all the necessary resources (people, time, funding) together to ensure that the decision or activity is carried out successfully. In many cases, an "R" might be seen as the project manager who does the planning; identifies who needs to be involved; communicates with others (that is, interfaces with "A's", "C's", and "I's"); influences others to attain the necessary help, resources, and information; and coordinates the work.

Approve

If a group or person has responsibility to "Approve" a decision or activity, then he or she has a "go/no-go" say in carrying it out (or not). While the "R's" may propose *how* to carry out the decision and *how* to do the work, the "A's" ultimately decide whether the plan will go forward. Therefore, the "A" in this case also stands for "accountable." The "A's" are ultimately accountable for the outcome of their decisions and the success of the work. It's important that "R's" engage "A's" early and often in their project planning to ensure their plans are on track. Likewise, "A's" should frequently check in with "R's" to monitor progress and ensure they have the information they need to make informed approvals or disapprovals. The relationship between the two individuals (or groups) should be one of constant communication and partnership.

Consult

If a person or group has this level of authority then they should be consulted prior to making decisions. "C's" work is significantly affected by "R's" work and "A's" final decisions. If "R" neglects to involve "C" early, this can lead to lack of "buy-in" for the critical decision or activity that "R" is trying to implement. Typically, "R" should consult with "C" prior to asking for "A's" approval because "C's" input may affect how "R" views the work/project and the primary decisions/approvals needed.

Inform

A group or person with this level of authority should be informed of the decision and other pertinent information that may affect him or her. "R" would typically be the one to inform "I" once "A" has approved the final decision or plan. The information may modestly affect what "I" is trying to accomplish, but it would not have nearly the impact that it does on "C."

Not Involved

As the label makes clear, these groups or individuals do not need to be involved and will not be affected at all by the decision or activity.

Clarifying roles and responsibilities not only defines when cooperation is necessary and what it looks like, but also reinforces the norm that cooperation is expected and appropriate. Another way to underscore that expectation is the presence of people who fit the description that Weber and Murnighan called "consistent contributors"—people who repeatedly cooperate in all situations and thus send a signal that cooperation is appropriate.

In their experiment, each participant was given 60 cents. They could choose to either keep the money or use it to buy a marker that yielded 40 cents for each group member, including themselves. As it turned out, members of groups that had consistent contributors made significantly more contributions to the "social good" than did members of groups without consistent contributors.

> Consistent contributors are catalysts for cooperation, especially among group members who are inclined to be cooperative but are unsure about what is appropriate. Such "uncertain" people want reassurance they will not be exploited if they contribute to establishing cooperative group norms, and the signals of consistent contributors provide that.[12]

Weber and Murnigham's findings should encourage us to "break the cycle" at work. To get cooperation you must demonstrate cooperation. If you or members of your team take the first step and model cooperative behavior, you'll increase the likelihood that the people you depend on to get work done will respond the same way. Through your behavior at work you can signal that cooperation is the expectation, encourage others to reciprocate in kind, and, when they do, demonstrate that they will not be taken advantage of.

Cooperation Builder 3: Align Interests and Establish Common Ground

Shared goals increase cooperation and collaboration because they ensure everyone is working toward the same outcome. When the objectives of one person or group are at odds with the objectives of another, efficiency and reliability suffer.

Picture the potential conflicts and inefficiencies that would result if one group in your unit was working toward reducing costs, while another group was focused on bringing state-of-the-art products and services to market. These objectives can coexist, but it most likely won't happen on its own. To facilitate alignment between the two groups, you need to develop compatible and mutually supportive objectives in a thoughtful and explicit manner.

One approach is to develop a set of broader, collective objectives for a team or work unit, then review the task objectives for specific individuals or groups and ensure that they are consistent with and mutually supportive of the collective objectives.

Here's an example: to set the stage at the beginning of the year, the chief technology officer of a large brokerage firm and his boss identify the ten critical objectives for the organization. These are goals that reflect its mission and are necessary for the overall success of the business enterprise. After the extended management team briefly reviews the goals, in-depth work is done to ensure that each will be accomplished.

Cross-functional teams discuss the goals in concurrent sessions to clarify, fine-tune, and determine what it will take to accomplish them, including key deliverables, help required, mileposts, key stakeholders, and so on. Following these discussions, the individual with primary accountability for a particular goal reports on the overall plan, identifies areas that require problem solving, and explains how progress and success will be monitored and communicated throughout the year.

After all the goals have been discussed, possible overlaps, synergies, tradeoffs and barriers are highlighted and resolved.

The process results in clarity among members of the extended team on priorities, resource allocation, and role expectations.

Disagreement Happens: How to Gain Support and Resolve Conflict

We've covered the importance of clear communication, clear roles, and shared goals. These conditions set the stage for cooperation and collaboration, but they alone are not sufficient. While they will provide a foundation to encourage cooperation and enable people to start to trust, they won't eliminate disagreements about what and how to do things—and they won't change the fact that we will make mistakes and fail to meet our co-workers' expectations.

Periodically, in order to sustain cooperation and collaboration, we need to gain the support of others for our ideas and constructively resolve differences.

Eleven Tactics for Influencing Others

Despite having shared goals in place, the people you depend on to get things done often have different perspectives on when and how to do them or even whether they should be done at all. In such instances you need to be able to gain their support and cooperation.

Several studies lead by Gary Yukl, an expert on leader effectiveness and the author of *Leadership in Organizations*, examined the relative effectiveness of individual influence tactics. Yukl has identified eleven proactive influence tactics, shown in Exhibit 7.2.[13]

Exhibit 7.2 Eleven Proactive Influence Tactics

Most-Effective Tactics

Rational Persuasion: Using logical arguments and factual evidence to show that a request or proposal is feasible and relevant for important task objectives.

Inspirational Appeals: Appealing to a person's values and ideals or seeking to arouse the person's emotions to gain commitment for a request or proposal.

Consultation: Asking the person to suggest improvements or help plan a proposed activity or change for which the person's support is desired.

Collaboration: Offering to provide relevant resources or assistance if the person will carry out a request or approve a proposed change.

Moderately Effective Tactics

Apprising: Explaining how carrying out a request or supporting a proposal will benefit the person personally or will help to advance the person's career.

Ingratiation: Using praise and flattery before or during an attempt to influence someone to carry out a request or support a proposal.

Personal Appeals: Asking the person to carry out a request or support a proposal out of friendship or asking for a personal favor before saying what it is.

Exchange: Offering something the person wants, or offering to reciprocate at a later time if the person will do what you request.

Least-Effective Tactics

Legitimating Tactics: Establishing the legitimacy of a request or verifying that you have the authority to make it.

Coalition Tactics: Enlisting the aid of others, or using the support of others as a way to influence someone to do something.

Pressure: Using demands, threats, frequent checking, or persistent reminders to influence someone to do something.

Four "core tactics" (the first four listed in the exhibit) have been found to be most effective at gaining commitment. They are *rational persuasion, inspirational appeals, consultation,* and *collaboration.*

Rational persuasion involves the use of explanations, logical arguments, and factual evidence to explain why a request or proposal will benefit the organization or help to achieve an objective (and, often, to explain why it's likely to be successful). Rational persuasion can be used for most types of influence attempts. It is most appropriate when the other person shares your objectives but does not recognize that the proposal is the best way to attain them.

Inspirational appeals involve an emotional or value-based argument, in contrast to the logical arguments used in rational persuasion. An inspirational appeal develops enthusiasm and commitment by arousing strong emotions and linking a request or proposal to a person's needs, values, hopes, and ideals. It may tap into her desire to feel useful, to develop and use her skills, to accomplish something worthwhile, to perform an exceptional feat, to be a member of the best team, or to participate in an exciting effort to make things better.

With *consultation* you invite the other person to participate in planning how to carry out a request or implement a proposed change. Consultation can involve different degrees of participation. The least amount of involvement occurs when you present a detailed proposal or plan and ask whether the other person has any doubts or concerns. After hearing his concerns, you can explain why they are unwarranted or modify the proposal to deal with them. Greater involvement occurs when you present a general strategy or objective and ask the other person to suggest specific action steps for implementing it. The suggested action steps are discussed until there is agreement by both parties.

Collaboration is a joint effort to accomplish the same task. It involves an offer to provide necessary resources and/or assistance if the other person will carry out a request or approve a proposal. Collaboration involves reducing the difficulty or costs of carrying out a request, and it is especially appropriate when compliance would be difficult for the other person.

Ingratiation, exchange, and *apprising* are moderately effective for influencing direct reports and peers, but they are difficult to use with your boss. *Personal appeals* can be useful for influencing a person with whom you have a friendly relationship. However, this tactic is only relevant for certain types of requests (for example, to get assistance, to ask for a personal favor, to change a scheduled meeting or deadline), and it is likely to result in compliance rather than commitment.

Pressure and *legitimating tactics* are not likely to result in commitment, but these tactics can be useful for eliciting compliance, and sometimes that's all you need to accomplish your objective. A *coalition* can be effective for influencing a peer or boss to support a change or innovation, especially if the coalition partners use direct tactics such as rational persuasion and inspirational appeals. However, use of a coalition is not likely to be effective if it involves pressure and is viewed as an attempt to "gang up" on the person.

Each type of influence tactic can be useful in the appropriate situation. Some tactics tend to be more effective than others, but the best tactics do not always result in commitment and the worst tactics do not always result in resistance. The outcome of an influence attempt is strongly affected by other factors as well, for example, your power and authority, your objective and expected outcome, the perceived importance of the request, the relationship between you and the other person, and cultural values and norms about the use of the tactics.

Any tactic can result in resistance if it is not used in a skillful manner or if it's used for an improper or unethical request. Factors that support and inhibit the use of each of the eleven influence tactics are summarized in Table 7.1.

Table 7.1 Factors Affecting the Choice of Tactics

Most Effective Tactics		
Influence Tactic	Supporting Factors	Limiting Factors
Simple Request	• Your request is clearly legitimate, relevant for the work, and something the person knows how to do.	• Your request is unpleasant, inconvenient, irrelevant, or difficult to do.
Rational Persuasion	• You and the person share task objectives. • You are seen as an expert. • You have a track record of success. • Can be used effectively with boss, peers, and direct reports.	• You have a poor track record in areas related to the request or proposal. • You are not seen a credible expert in areas relevant to the request or proposal. • The other person is considered an expert in areas relevant to request or proposal.
Inspirational Appeals	• Most effective with direct reports and peers. • Objective is to gain commitment to work on a new project or support for a proposed change. • You know the person's values and what motivates him or her.	• The person is the boss. • You have a poor personal relationship with the person. • The person lacks trust and/or respect for you. • You do not know the person very well or what motivates him or her.

Table 7.1 (*Continued*)

Most-Effective Tactics		
Influence Tactic	Supporting Factors	Limiting Factors
Consultation	• Most effective with direct reports and peers. • You have the authority to assign work or make changes. • The person's cooperation is needed for effective implementation. • The person has relevant information that you do not. • The person agrees in principle with the objective.	• You have a poor relationship with the person. • The person is not willing to be open and provide suggestions or raise concerns. • The person does not have the expertise to make a meaningful contribution. • The person's cooperation is not necessary for successful implementation.
Collaboration	• Most effective with peers. • You can provide additional resources to help the person. • You can reduce the difficulty or cost of carrying out a request.	• The person is the boss. • You do not have any way to reduce difficulty or unpleasantness of carrying out the request. • You cannot avoid creating a new problem and reduce the cost of compliance.

(*continued overleaf*)

Table 7.1 (*Continued*)

Moderately Effective Tactics		
Influence Tactic	Supporting Factors	Limiting Factors
Apprising	• More effective with direct reports and peers. • You have knowledge about the benefits that would result from the person's compliance.	• The person is the boss. • You are new to the organization and person is experienced. • You do not know what the person values.
Ingratiation	• More effective with direct reports and peers. • You have positive relationship with the person. • Best when used regularly and not just before the initial request.	• The person is the boss. • The person does not hold you in very high regard. • You only use tactic before you make a request. • The person has already expressed resistance to first request.
Personal Appeals	• More effective with peers. • Request involves a personal favor. • You know the person well; you have a friendly relationship. • The person is loyal to you. • You have done previous favors for the person.	• Person is the boss or a direct report. • You and the person do not know each other very well. • You and the person do not get along very well. • You have not reciprocated for previous favors done by the person.

Table 7.1 (Continued)

Moderately Effective Tactics		
Influence Tactic	Supporting Factors	Limiting Factors
Exchange	• More effective with direct reports and peers. • You understand what the person wants and values. • You control incentives the person desires. • The person is not being asked to do something he or she feels is unpleasant or inconvenient.	• The person is the boss. • You do not know what the person wants or values. • You have a poor track record of returning favors. • Better used to build cooperative relationships.
Least-Effective Tactics		
Influence Tactic	Supporting Factors	Limiting Factors
Legitimating	• Perceived outcome stakes are high for you. • Other influence tactics have been tried without success. • The person is unfamiliar with relevant policies, agreements, or standard practices. • Your authority to make a request is not well defined.	• Request is consistent with your authority. • The person recognizes your right to make the request.

(continued overleaf)

Table 7.1 (Continued)

Least-Effective Tactics		
Influence Tactic	Supporting Factors	Limiting Factors
Coalition Building	• More effective with peers and bosses. • You do not have direct access to the person. • You are not seen as credible by the person you are trying to influence. • Works best as follow-up to other tactics. • Seldom used alone.	• The person is a direct report. • You are perceived to be credible by the person. • You have experience and expertise relevant to the request or proposal. • Lack of trust in your motives causes the person to view attempt as coercive.
Pressure	• "Hard" form of tactic can be effective with a direct reports. • "Soft" form of tactic can be effective with peers. • Perceived outcome stakes are high for you. • Other influence tactics have been tried without success. • You can monitor compliance. • You have the power to deliver consequences for non-compliance.	• The person is the boss or someone with more power and authority. • You and the person need to work together frequently and cooperate to get work done.

Manage Differences and Reach Agreement

Encouraging collaboration between individuals, departments, and teams is the key to execution and getting things done. However, there is a drawback to throwing more opinions and perspectives into the mix: the potential for disagreement increases dramatically. Indeed, the potential for conflict is created the moment individuals or teams begin to do their work.

The word "conflict" often conjures up images of confrontation and major disagreement, but this is frequently not the case. Rather, the word (at least the way I'm using it) describes any disagreement—and you'll find disagreements in even the most positive and productive work relationship. At least, you *should*. Many people avoid or minimize conflicts in an attempt to maintain harmonious relationships. This is a mistake because conflict itself is inherently neither good nor bad. What is positive or negative is how the differences are managed and the outcome that results.[14]

Positive and Negative Effects of Conflict. When you bring conflict to the surface, you can address the problem and take action to resolve it. If you ignore conflict or try to gloss over it or cover it up, the problem many never be resolved. And while not all problems can be resolved to everyone's satisfaction, recognizing that conflict exists and attempting to deal with it is preferable to ignoring it.

Sometimes, more than one issue is involved in a particular conflict. People may not "see the forest for the trees" because of hidden disagreements over intangibles such as status and self-esteem. Often, the underlying conflict must be addressed before the more obvious problem can be dealt with effectively. Thus, the process of resolving a pending conflict may help resolve long-standing issues as well.

Dealing with disagreements before they have a chance to grow can help the people involved more effectively resolve their problems in the future. Many a solid long-term relationship is born from the difficult but constructive resolution of a conflict.

Productive conflict management can also foster creativity. To resolve a problem, people are often required to search for alternative solutions. This stimulates creative thinking and requires the use of interpersonal skills. People who have resolved a disagreement often say something like, "Well, I'm glad we've finally gotten that out in the open. I never saw it that way before."

However, not all conflict has a positive outcome. If it's not managed well, it can have serious negative effects. For instance, it's been said that "knowledge is power" and some people may become reluctant to share information for fear that the other person may use that knowledge to "get the upper hand." It is extremely difficult to work cooperatively in an atmosphere of distrust. Often, poor results are obtained—or perhaps no results at all.

When there are no productive results from an attempt to resolve conflict, the conflict often intensifies and the need for resolution becomes more urgent. The people involved still need to resolve the original issue, but the atmosphere is less constructive. In any conflict situation, it's important not to "win the battle, but lose the war." If one person wins but seriously harms the long-term relationship with the others, victory may be short-lived. The point? Any disagreement should be resolved in a way that minimizes the negative effect on future interactions.

The Four Basic Conflict Issues. Differences of opinion concerning one or more of the following four issues will cause conflict to occur: *facts, methods, goals,* and *values.*

Differences of *fact* are the most straightforward conflicts to resolve. After all, facts are concrete. They can be checked, compared, and tested, and this provides a basis for discussion and the exchange of information. Conflicts over facts can be resolved through dialogue more often than conflicts involving the other basic issues.

Let's say, for example, that a team is developing an action plan, and a conflict arises over the length of time needed to do a particular step. The conflict can be resolved by finding and discussing specific data related to the time required for that step as well as identifying any other conditions that may alter the timetable.

Methods are the second issue over which a conflict may arise. People may have similar goals and agree on the facts, but may be unable to agree on ways to achieve their goals. However, the presence of similar goals means that a logical, rational way of choosing among alternative approaches is possible. It's just a matter of convincing everyone that a particular method will achieve the goals at hand.

To illustrate, Carlos and Michael are two production managers trying to rework an assembly-line process, and each prefers a different method for accomplishing the goal. At meetings each promotes his preferred method with little progress toward agreement—until they realize they share the goal of improving assembly-line efficiency. Once this common ground is established, the two managers are able to look at each method more objectively. It now becomes a matter of reviewing the facts to determine which method does the best job. And because Carlos and Michael have a shared goal they can focus on finding the method that "is the best" rather than on the one they "like the best."

When the issue is related to *goals*, people have different objectives and may be supporting different courses of action. Information sharing is the key to resolving conflicts over either methods or goals. It helps each person understand what is important to the other person.

Occasionally, when differing goals exist, a third person may be needed to determine which goal (or combination of goals) is most appropriate.

For example, a cereal company's marketing group wants a package redesigned in a certain way to make it more attractive and to increase sales. The distribution group feels the new design will lead to breakage problems and will affect their quality standards. Once each group understands the needs and goals of the other, both can focus on developing a solution that works for everyone (in this case a redesign that was more attractive and did not create breakage problems). If they are unable to find a solution that meets the goal of both groups, they may need to involve the product manager to clarify which goal has the higher priority.

Conflicts arising from different values are most difficult to resolve. In fact, they are often unresolvable. People's beliefs tend to become inflexible over long periods of time, and they are often based on emotion rather than on reason. Finding common ground and separating the unresolvable from the resolvable frequently moves such conflicts toward productive action.

For example, Linda, the general manager of a manufacturing company, feels that it's inappropriate to have alcoholic beverages at the annual picnic. Most of the team members feel that, since it *is* their picnic, they should have the right to determine the way the picnic fund is used. This conflict is almost impossible to resolve without creating some ill will or resentment because it is based on personal preferences and beliefs. If, however, a conflict is related to the core values of the organization, the organizational core values should override individual preferences.

> Neglected conflicts have a tendency to grow. Generally speaking, a conflict left unresolved or unattended will morph from a conflict over facts, methods, or goals into a conflict over values — and in turn will become increasingly difficult to resolve. You can see why it's best to address conflicts head-on the minute they begin to take shape.

Figure 7.1 Five Conflict Management Styles

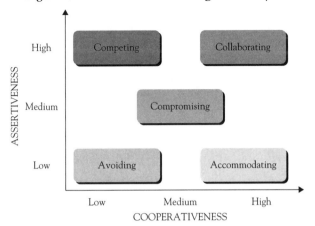

Based on Thomas & Kilmann, 1974

Five Styles for Managing Conflict. Conflict is managed through a combination of assertiveness and cooperativeness (see Figure 7.1). *Assertiveness* is defined as behaviors that are used to meet your own needs. *Cooperativeness* is defined as behaviors that are used to meet the needs of others. These two dimensions of behavior are not mutually exclusive—for example, you can work toward getting your needs met and, at the same time, work toward helping the person with whom you have a difference of opinion get her needs met—and yield five distinct conflict management styles.[15]

The most important thing to understand is that no style is "good" or "bad." Any style can be effective when used in the appropriate situation. Table 7.2 shows the advantages and disadvantages of each style and when each style would be most effective.

Factors That Influence Behavior During a Conflict. Most people have a primary and a secondary conflict management style that they are effective and comfortable using.[16] The key to being able to productively manage conflict is your ability to use all five

Table 7.2 Advantages and Disadvantages of Each Conflict Style

	Description	When Useful	Advantages	Disadvantages
AVOID	• Ignore; refuse to take a stand; walk away. • Wait and hope.	• When your stake is not high and when confrontation would damage a critical relationship.	• Avoids or postpones confrontation. • May maintain relationships that would be hurt by confrontation.	• Does not eliminate the conflict. • May mean leaving situation to chance. • Overuse can intensify conflict.
ACCOMMODATE	• Do what the other person wants. • Try to cover up. • Pretend everything is okay. • Lose-win.	• When issue is minor. • When maintaining relationship is primary consideration. • When goals are aligned.	• Relationships are maintained. • Allows time to obtain more information. • Allows time for feelings to cool down.	• Temporary fix, not resolution of conflict. • May be counter-productive. • Overuse may lead others to take advantage of you. • May not meet your needs.

194

Table 7.2 (*Continued*)

	Description	When Useful	Advantages	Disadvantages
COMPROMISE	• Bargain. • Negotiate. • Give-and-take. • "Split the difference." • Partial win/partial lose for both.	• When issue is complex and critical, no clear or simple solution. • When parties have a strong stake in different solutions.	• Conflict can be resolved quickly. • Relationships can be maintained. • Each party gains something.	• Each party loses or gives something up; can lead to sub-optimum solutions. • Ill feelings may remain. • Overuse may lead to game-playing.
COMPETE	• Battle. • Autocratic; aggressive. • Satisfy own needs at the expense of others. • Win-lose.	• When immediate action is required. • When maintaining relationship is not critical. • When conflict is over personal differences that won't change.	• Allows parties to move on. • Sometimes decisions are better than those arrived at by compromise.	• Leads to development of negative feelings (hostility, resentment) between conflicting parties. • Most often associated with negative outcomes.

(*continued overleaf*)

Table 7.2 (Continued)

	Description	When Useful	Advantages	Disadvantages
COLLABORATE	• Confront root cause. • Problem-solve. • Win-win.	• Situations with long-term implications. • When maintaining relationship is important. • Peer conflicts. • When time permits.	• The only strategy clearly related to positive outcomes in a wide range of circumstances.	• Requires commitment and hard work from both parties. • May take more time than other approaches.

styles effectively and flexibly based on the conflict situation. In other words, you must be able to analyze a conflict situation to determine what style it calls for and use behaviors appropriate to that style.

First, you'll need to assess situational factors such as time pressures and the individual characteristics of the people involved. Table 7.3 summarizes the factors that influence behavior and determine which conflict management style is most appropriate. These situational variables affect your desire and ability to be assertive and cooperative. This, in turn, affects the probable success of the style used to manage a conflict.

Let's define a few terms. *Outcome stakes* are each person's or group's views of what they stand to win or lose. Gains or losses can be both personal and organizational. This interaction between organizational and personal stakes has a strong effect on the perceptions of the overall importance of the outcome. The belief that there is either a lot or a little "on the line" affects the extent to which you feel it is desirable to focus on your needs and objectives at the expense of the other person's (to be more or less assertive, in other words).

For example, a manager fears losing control over the development of the computer systems for a division. The outcome stakes are high for him personally because he feels his career is on the line. In this situation he may be more motivated to focus on his needs and goals than on the needs and goals of the other people involved.

Relative power refers to the authority inherent in a person's position, control of information or control of rewards and punishments, the quality of relationships with the other person (which comes from one person's high regard for the other), or expertise such as the relevant knowledge, skills, or experience brought to the situation. Your power relative to the other people involved in the conflict determines how feasible it is for you to be assertive and focus on getting your own needs met.

Table 7.3 Factors That Influence Behavior During Conflict

Situation	Most Effective Behavior	Style
HIGH levels of Outcome Stakes and Relative Power LOW levels of Interest Interdependence and Relationship Quality	HIGH levels of Assertiveness + LOW levels of Cooperativeness	= COMPETING
LOW levels of Outcome Stakes and Relative Power HIGH levels of Interest Interdependence and Relationship Quality	LOW levels of Assertiveness + HIGH levels of Cooperativeness	= ACCOMMODATING
LOW levels of Outcome Stakes and Relative Power LOW levels of Interest Interdependence and Relationship Quality	LOW levels of Assertiveness + LOW levels of Cooperativeness	= AVOIDING
HIGH levels of Outcome Stakes and Relative Power HIGH levels of Interest Interdependence and Relationship Quality	HIGH levels of Assertiveness + HIGH levels of Cooperativeness	= COLLABORATING

In conflict situations in which you don't know or haven't worked with the other person or group involved, role-related power tends to play a larger part. Over time, however—as conflicts between the people or groups are resolved and relationships develop—relationship and expertise may balance the relative power between the people or groups. Let's say, for instance, that a purchasing agent (Sue) is working on a contract with a lawyer (Agnes) who must approve it before it can be signed. Since Sue has worked successfully with Agnes on previous contracts, she feels she can get Agnes to approve the contract.

Common ground (interest interdependence) involves shared goals and/or methods for attaining them. When interest interdependence is high and people depend on each other to get the work done, it affects the desirability of being cooperative in a conflict situation. Imagine an information technology group that has a large number of projects to complete but limited resources and time. It's easy to see why they would want to work together to set priorities and allocate resources to ensure that projects are done in a timely way and meet customer expectations.

Relationship quality is based on perceptions and past experience. Good ones involve factors such as credibility, respect, trust, caring about the other person's needs, following through on commitments, and "walking the talk." Initial perceptions can change (for better or worse) as people interact over time. A good relationship increases the feasibility of cooperation and a bad relationship decreases it.

For example, Joe and Barbara, the vice presidents of two business units, plan to enter into a joint venture. They have worked together before and the results have been excellent for both businesses. Pricing and distribution of profits are discussed openly as each vice president works to meet the needs of both business units and the goals of the organization.

Time pressure also impacts the dynamics and behaviors of conflict resolution. Often, due to time pressure, people will lower their expectations to gain a partial achievement of their goals.

Interest interdependence increases if everyone is under the same time constraints. If only one person is under time pressure, interest interdependence is considerably lowered. In such situations the person with more formal authority may resort to using it to obtain his or her goals.

Here's an example: Esther, a department manager, is seeking to hire a replacement. She is being very selective because of the great amount of time required to train the replacement. However, Esther's manager, Sinclair, wants her to hire immediately. Because he anticipates an increase in demand during the upcoming holiday season, Sinclair would like to see the position filled right away. Although he would normally support Esther's desire to use a more deliberate process, he feels the need to have the position filled is too important and he asks her to accelerate the process and make the hire ASAP.

Managing Conflict Productively. In general, to manage differences effectively, your mindset should be that people have the right to think or feel differently than you do and that it is to your benefit to develop solutions that will be acceptable and beneficial to everyone concerned. In a less-than-ideal world, however, people don't always hold that mindset.

> Here are a few mistakes people commonly make when trying to resolve conflicts:
>
> - Minimizing or ignoring others' concerns
> - Pulling power plays
> - Attacking the legitimacy of the other person's position or priorities
> - Suppressing differences

- Imposing their own goals/priorities
- Refusing to temporarily remove constraints
- Going through the motions of managing the difference, but refusing to carry it through

So how, exactly, should you manage conflict? It's best to clarify the situation by identifying the individuals involved in the conflict, identify the specific issues, and gather facts and perceptions of the people involved. A seven-step process for managing conflict can be applied to most situations:

1. Describe what's important to you and why.
2. Check your understanding of what's important to the other person and why.
3. Identify common ground and look for points of interdependence.
4. Invite alternatives that address your needs/goals and those of the other person.
5. Use active listening (paraphrase, questions, balanced response) to evaluate alternatives, resolve concerns, and improve ideas.
6. If an alternative isn't immediately available, temporarily remove constraints to invite and propose new alternatives.
7. End the discussion by summarizing key points and stating next steps.

The checklist in Exhibit 7.3 summarizes the main things you should consider when faced with a conflict. It can help you analyze the situation and plan how best to resolve it.

Exhibit 7.3 What to Consider When Faced with Conflict

Describe the basic conflict issue.

_____

_____

❏ Facts   ❏ Methods   ❏ Goals   ❏ Values

What are your needs/goals?

_____

_____

What are the other person's/group's needs/goals?

_____

_____

Factors That Influence Conflict

What are the stakes involved from your perspective and the other person's perspective?

_____

_____

What is your relative power in the conflict?

_____

_____

To what extent does common ground exist?

_____

_____

How would you describe your relationship with the other person?

_____

_____

What kinds of time pressure do you face?

_____

_____

Approach for Resolving the Conflict

What is your primary style (competing, collaborating, compromising, avoiding, or accommodating)?

_____

_____

What is the other person's primary style?

_____

_____

What should your style be (more or less assertive/cooperative)?

_____

_____

What should the other person's style be?

_____

_____

What factors can be changed, added, or subtracted to move the conflict to a productive outcome? How?

_____

What are some specific next steps?

_____

The Bottom Line

Organizations are complex structures with many interdependencies. We must rely on others to help get things done and meet our objectives, and that means cooperation and collaboration are often the key to our success. While there is evidence that human beings base our actions on self-interest in an effort to maximize personal benefit, ample evidence also supports the proposition that our natural inclination is toward cooperation. The challenge you face in the workplace is to ensure the conditions that create and sustain cooperation and collaboration are in place.

Cooperation and collaboration are facilitated by clear communication, shared goals, and clearly defined roles. These conditions help encourage and motivate people to focus on the group's best interest without feeling that they are minimizing or trading off their own interests in the process. Once in place, however, cooperation is a delicate state. People will still have disagreements and different points of view about how and when things should happen. Your ability to effectively and constructively influence others and gain their support is critical to maintaining cooperation. The loss of cooperation is also caused by mistakes and miscommunication, and it can be undermined if naturally occurring and healthy disagreements are not well managed.

We do know that when you act in a cooperative manner it causes others to reciprocate. It often comes down to a willingness to break the cycle of competition with one person or group taking the risk of the first step.

Conclusion: Five Lessons
for Leaders

If you've stayed with me to this point, I hope you've learned some tactics you can put into practice today and in the future. And now I'd like to ask you to step back from the nitty-gritty details of execution and take at broader look at some "big picture" principles.

The survey results that inspired this book point to five general lessons for leaders who are trying to enhance their ability to execute plans and initiatives and deliver consistent results. These broader "themes" came out of our study and they relate (sometimes directly and other times indirectly) to the topics that I've covered in the previous pages.

Lesson 1: Integrate the Leader and Manager Roles

Successful execution depends on the ability of individuals to integrate the leader and manager roles. You've doubtless heard that *leading* (traditionally defined as formulating a vision and strategy and engaging employees) and *managing* (traditionally defined as attending to the operational issues related to execution) are both important skills. Our study confirms this belief. Yet all too often, the leader and manager roles are artificially split, causing people to think of themselves as one or the other.

It appears that organizations that are better at execution have leaders who can look to the future and prepare the business to adapt to changes in the environment as well as skillfully attend to the granular issues of implementation. The implication is clear: you and other members of your company need both skills. The real challenge is to understand when each role is most appropriate and be able to excel at both.

Lesson 2: Clarify Assumptions and Priorities

Many businesses put a lot of energy into crafting their vision and strategy and gaining agreement on them. However, it seems they take less time clarifying assumptions about what it will take to achieve the strategy and set priorities for action. Everyone may agree that it's important for their company to be innovative or efficient. Problem is, everyone may *not* agree on what "innovative" or "efficient" actually looks like.

The point? Your company must go beyond developing a shared picture of its strategic direction and articulate key assumptions and priorities related to execution. Spell out exactly what needs to happen ... and exactly when, where, how, and by whom. This increases the likelihood that more detailed implementation plans will be targeted toward outcomes that have the greatest impact. For less-successful companies, this step is frequently missing.

Lesson 3: Make Sure the Right Systems Are in Place

Execution is not just about leader behavior. Organizational structure and management systems must support and reinforce that behavior. If, for example, your strategy calls for "innovation," are systems in place to facilitate organizational learning and creative thinking? Or do you just *assume* (and you know the pitfalls of assuming!) it's sufficient to ask leaders to make them happen?

To encourage innovation, you need a mechanism for screening and funding new ideas. Your employees shouldn't have to struggle to find support and resources to bring their brainstorms to fruition.

People always cite the efforts of Art Fry and Spencer Silver, the 3M employees who invented the Post-it® Note, as a shining success story of personal initiative and perseverance. They worked outside the system and used ingenuity to keep their project alive.

But here's what I want to know: Why did those guys have to work so hard? Wouldn't it have been better for everyone if a support system *had* been in place? And how many other fantastically lucrative ideas fell by the wayside because that system wasn't there?

In addition, the most successful organizations ensure there is a proper balance of centralized and decentralized responsibility, and that people at all levels have the freedom to take actions to achieve results. This improves responsiveness, accountability, and allows change issues to be managed right where they happen.

Lesson 4: Coordinate and Monitor High-Impact Actions

It's generally understood that vision and strategy must be translated into action at each level of the organization. But the most successful companies go beyond that. Their managers ensure that these actions are mutually supportive and well coordinated across departments and levels—rather than letting everyone do what they think is best for their department or division—and monitor them to ensure that performance expectations are met.

Actually, monitoring may be one of the most critical aspects of the strategy execution process. It's how companies make change stick. People tend to lose momentum otherwise, quickly reverting to "business as usual." The most successful companies are consistent and persistent in monitoring and reinforcing their strategic actions. They recalibrate the plan when new information becomes available.

Lesson 5: Get Change Management Right

Volumes have been written about the importance of managing change. Despite that, we found that managers get low marks in this area. Yes, managers can be trained to recognize the various phases of transition and commitment among employees, and they can learn what they should say and do at each stage to gain support for the change. Still, if they neglect key areas previously mentioned—coordinating decisions and actions across levels and departments and ensuring that organizational structures and systems that facilitate execution are in place—people *will* perceive a strategy-execution gap. Worse, they will doubt that the organization can close that gap.

Of course, leader behavior also counts. What our study described as "involving people in decisions that affect them" *does* have a significant impact on people's perception of a leader's ability to manage change, as well as on the quality of execution and overall performance. Not surprisingly, given respondents' low opinion of management's ability to manage change effectively, "involving people" is one of the five lowest-rated items on our survey. Change that reality and you can help your company make better decisions and gain stronger buy-in. This, in turn, will have a positive impact on the effectiveness of the change process and the ability to execute strategies.

The Bottom Line

Execution is hard. And if you're like many people, it's not a skill you were born with. The good news? It *is* a skill you can learn and refine. What does it take to reach the point at which you feel competent in your ability to effectively execute and consistently get things done? The answer is both simple and difficult—*practice* and *time*.

According to two well-known writers—Malcolm Gladwell, author of *Outliers: The Story of Success*, and Geoff Colvin, author of *Talent Is Overrated: What Really Separates World-Class Performers from Everybody Else*—practice is what makes the difference between those who are good at something and those who are great. It's not some innate ability. According to both authors, success in any area is the result of hard work and consistently putting in the time—plain and simple.

Yet, as straightforward as this sounds, there is a twist. The people who go on to be great don't just focus on the things they are already good at—they spend most of their time working on the things they are *not yet* good at.

For me, this is a message of hope. It's reassuring to know that no matter what your current capability, with practice you can reach a high level of competence. And this is the message I'd like to leave you with. Start today and put in the time. Use the tools and techniques outlined in this book. It might not go as well as you'd like the first few times, but hang in there. Use each attempt as an opportunity to learn. Take that learning and use it to do better the next time. Try, learn, do it again, and keep at it—that's the winning formula.

Appendix

Criteria for Identifying Top-Performing and Less-Successful Companies

Respondents were asked to provide performance data on their organizations. Specifically, they were asked to indicate the percentage each item increased or decreased over the past three years based on the following scale:

1 = Decreased more than 10 percent

2 = Decreased between 6 and 10 percent

3 = Decreased between 1 and 5 percent

4 = Stayed constant

5 = Increased between 1 and 5 percent

6 = Increased between 6 and 10 percent

7 = Increased more than 10 percent

? = Don't know

A performance composite score was calculated for each respondent based on reported company net sales and net earnings. This composite score ranged on a scale from 1 to 7, with 1 being least successful and 7 being most successful.

Respondents with composite scores of 7.0 were considered top performing (N = 82), and those with scores <5 were considered less successful (N = 79). The distribution of composite scores among the less-successful companies was as follows:

Composite Score	Number of Respondent Companies
1.00	2
1.50	4
2.00	5
2.50	5
3.00	13
3.50	11
4.00	23
4.50	16

The distribution across industries was consistent with the overall respondent population:

Industry	Top Performing: Number of Respondent Companies	Less Successful: Number of Respondent Companies
Pharmaceuticals and Chemicals	12	6
Healthcare/Medical	14	26
Financial Services	26	11
Insurance	9	6
Manufacturing	21	30
TOTAL	82	79

Because of our confidentiality agreement, we are not able to provide the names of the companies that participated in the study.

Notes

Chapter Two: Bridge Builder 1:
Translate Strategy into Action

1. Wall, S. J. *On the fly: Executing strategy in a changing world.* Hoboken, NJ: John Wiley & Sons, 2004.

Chapter Three: Bridge Builder 2:
Expect Top Performance

1. Rosenthal, R., & Jacobson, L. *Pygmalion in the classroom: Teacher expectations and pupils intellectual development.* New York: Holt, Rinehart & Winston, 1968.
2. Eden, D., & Shani, A. B. Pygmalion goes to boot camp: Expectancy, leadership, and trainee performance. *Journal of Applied Psychology*, 1982, 67, 194–199.
3. King, A. S. Self-fulfilling prophecies in training the hard-core: Supervisors' expectations and the underprivileged workers' performance. *Social Science Quarterly*, 1971, 52, 369–378.
4. Eden, D. *Pygmalion in management: Productivity as a self-fulfilling prophecy.* Lexington, MA: Lexington Books, 1990.
5. Rosenthal, R., & Rubin, D. B. Interpersonal expectations effects: The first 345 studies. *Behavioral and Brain Science*, 1978, 3, 377–386.

6. Eden, D. *Pygmalion in management: Productivity as a self-fulfilling prophecy.* Lexington, MA: Lexington Books, 1990.
7. LaBarre, Polly. Marcus Buckingham thinks your boss has an attitude problem. *Fast Company,* August 2001, p. 88.
8. The model was developed by the Center for Creative Leadership. ©Center for Creative Leadership. All Rights Reserved.

Chapter Four: Bridge Builder 3: Hold People Accountable

1. Loomis, C. J. Robert Rubin on the job he never wanted. *Fortune,* November 26, 2007, *156*(11), 68.
2. Williams, C. Tyson Gay eliminated after finishing fifth in semi. *McClatchy Newspapers,* August 16, 2008.
3. Patrick, D. USA is still on track to lead medal haul. *USA Today,* August 22, 2008.
4. Lerner, J. S., & Tetlock, P. E. Accounting for the effects of accountability. *Psychological Bulletin,* 1999, *125,* 255–275.
5. Tetlock, P. Accountability and the perseverance of first impressions. *Social Psychology Quarterly,* 1983, *46,* 74–83.
6. Fandt, P. M. The relationship of accountability and interdependent behavior to enhancing team consequences. *Group & Organization Studies,* 1991, *16,* 300–312.
7. Fern, B., & Cohen, H. *Leading for employee engagement.* Bedford, NY: Performance Connections International, Inc., 2006.
8. Clarey, C. A weekend warrior falls in a spate of mistakes. *The New York Times,* July 18, 2009, p. D1.
9. Clark, A., & Treanor, J. Greenspan. I was wrong about the economy—sort of. *The Guardian,* October 24, 2008.
10. Murphy, S. Molnau and her aide fling blame, deflect responsibility. *Minneapolis Star Tribune,* November 27, 2007.
11. You might think Lehman Bros. Fuld would be chastened. *Financial Times,* October 8, 2008

12. Markman, K. D., & Tetlock, P. E. I couldn't have known: Accountability, foreseeability, and counterfactual denials of responsibility. *British Journal of Social Psychology*, 2000, 39, 313–325.

13. Williams, K. D., Nida, S. A., Baca, D. L., & Latane, B. Social loafing and swimming: Effects of identifiability on individual and relay performance of intercollegiate swimmers. *Basic and Applied Social Psychology*, 1989, 10(1), 73–81.

14. Markman, K. D., & Tetlock, P. E. I couldn't have known: Accountability, foreseeability, and counterfactual denials of responsibility. *British Journal of Social Psychology*, 2000, 39, 313–325.

15. Watkins, S. Finding a job, but moving a family. *The New York Times*, July 26, 2009, p. 8.

16. Steinhauer, J. Gunman kills 1 and wounds 5 at Florida office. *The New York Times*, November 7, 2009, p. A12.

17. Fern, B., & Cohen, H. *Leading for employee engagement.* Bedford, NY: Performance Connections International, Inc., 2006.

18. Ibid.

19. Ibid

Chapter Five: Bridge Builder 4: Involve the Right People in Making the Right Decisions

1. Weiser, Charles R. Best practice in customer relations. *Consumer Policy Review*, July, 1994.

2. Nelson, Bob. Worker ideas can improve the bottom line. *Business First-Columbus*, May 25, 2001, p. A21.

3. Sanfey, A. G., Loewenstein, G., McClure, S. M., & and Cohen, J. D. Neuroeconomics: Cross-currents in research on decision making. *TRENDS in Cognitive Science*, 2006, 10(3), 108–116.

4. Ibid.

5. Norris, F. Most failing banks are doing it the old-school way. *The New York Times*, August 21, 2009, p. B1.
6. Klein, G. *Sources of power: How people make decisions.* Cambridge, MA: The MIT Press, 1998.
7. Bechara, B. The role of emotion in decision making: Evidence from neurological patients with orbitofrontal damage. *Brain and Cognition*, 2004, *55*, 30–40.
8. Ibid.
9. Sanfey, A. G., Loewenstein, G., McClure, S. M., & Cohen, J. D. Neuroeconomics: Cross-currents in research on decision making. *TRENDS in Cognitive Science*, 2006, *10*(3), 108–116.
10. Kuhnen, C. M., & and Knutson, B. The neural basis of financial risk taking. *Neuron*, 2005, *47*, 763–770.
11. Bechara, B., Damasio, A. R., Damasio, H., & Anderson, S. W. Insensitivity to future consequences following damage to human prefrontal cortex. *Cognition*, 1994, *50*, 7–15.
12. Vroom, V. H., & and Jago, A. G. *The new leadership.* Englewood Cliffs, New Jersey: Prentice-Hall, 1988.
13. Vroom, V. H., & and Yetton, P. *Leadership and decision making.* Pittsburg, PA: University of Pittsburg Press: 1973.
14. Yukl, G. *Skills for managers and leaders: Texts, cases, and exercises.* Englewood Cliffs, New Jersey: Prentice-Hall, 1990.
15. Ibid.
16. Kepner, C. H., & and Tregoe, B. B. *The rational manager: A systematic approach to problem solving and decision making* (1st ed.). New York: McGraw-Hill, 1965.
17. Klein, G. *Sources of power: How people make decisions.* Cambridge, MA: The MIT Press, 1998.

Chapter Six: Bridge Builder 5: Facilitate Change Readiness

1. Lepsinger, R., & Forgie, J. *The secrets of successful change: How top performing companies prepare for and manage change.* New York: OnPoint Consulting, 2006.

2. Prochaska, J. O., Norcross, J. C., & DiClemente, C. C. *Change for good: A revolutionary six-stage program for overcoming bad habits and moving your life positively forward.* New York: HarperCollins, 1994.
3. Ibid.
4. Ibid.
5. Ibid.
6. Ibid.
7. Fern, B., & Cohen, H. *Leading for employee engagement.* Bedford, NY: Performance Connections International, Inc., 2006.
8. Patterson, G. R., & Forgatch, M. S. Therapist behavior as a determinant for client noncompliance: A paradox for the behavior modifier. *Journal of Consulting and Clinical Psychology,* 1985, *53*(6), 846–851.
9. Ibid.
10. Miller, W. R., & Rollnick, S. Talking oneself into change: Motivational interviewing, stages of change, and therapeutic process. *Journal of Cognitive Psychotherapy,* 2004, *18*(4), 299–308.
11. Ibid.
12. Fern, B., & Cohen, H. *Leading for employee engagement.* Bedford, NY: Performance Connections International, Inc., 2006.
13. Lepsinger, R., & Forgie, J. *The secrets of successful change: How top performing companies prepare for and manage change.* New York: OnPoint Consulting, 2006.

Chapter Seven: Bridge Builder 6: Increase Coordination and Cooperation

1. Hardin, G. The tragedy of the commons. *Science,* 1968, *162,* 1243–1248.
2. Nowak, M. A., & Sigmund, K. Cooperation versus competition. *Financial Analyst Journal,* July/August 2000, pp. 13–22.

3. Ibid.

4. Canegallo, C., Ortona, G., Ottone, S., Ponzano, F., & Scacciati, F. Competition versus cooperation: Some experimental evidence. *The Journal of Socio-Economics*, 2008, *37*, 18–30.

5. Mead, M. *Cooperation and competition among primitive people* (1st ed.). New York and London: McGraw-Hill, 1937.

6. Ibid.

7. Rilling, J. J., Gutman, D. A., Zeh, T. R., Pagnoni, G., Berns, G. S., & Kits, C. D. A neural basis for social cooperation. *Neuron*, 2002, *35*, 395–405.

8. Weber, J. M., & Murnighan, J. K. Suckers or saviors? Consistent contributors in social dilemmas. *Journal of Personality and Social Psychology*, 2008, p. 134.

9. Monterosso, J., Ainslie, G., Toppi Mullen, P. A.-C. P., & Gault, B. The fragility of cooperation: A false feedback study of a sequential iterated prisoner's dilemma. *Journal of Economic Psychology*, 2002, *23*, 437–448.

10. Klein, G. *Sources of power: How people make decisions.* Cambridge, MA: The MIT Press, 1998.

11. Ibid.

12. Weber, J. M., & Murnighan, J. K. Suckers or saviors? Consistent contributors in social dilemmas. *Journal of Personality and Social Psychology*, 2008, p. 134.

13. Yukl, G., Seifert, C. F., & Chavez, C. Validation of the extended influence behavior questionnaire. *The Leadership Quarterly*, 2008, *19*, 609–621.

14. I would like to thank Harold Scharlatt for the significant contribution he has made in shaping my thinking in the area of productive conflict management.

15. Thomas, K. W., & Kilmann, R. H. *The conflict mode instrument.* Tuxedo, NY: Xicom, 1974.

16. Ibid.

Index

execution, 35–36; and standards of excellence, 36–38
Vroom, Victor, 112

W

"Wait and hope" syndrome, 80
Wal-Mart, 13–14
Watkins, Skip, 90

Weber, J. Mark, 171, 178
Williams, Kipling D., 88
Woods, Tiger, 83

Y

Yetton, Philip, 112
Yukl, Gary, 112; influence tactics, 180–188